THE EXECUTIVE STRATEGIST

THE EXECUTIVE

An Armchair Guide to Scientific Decision-making

ROBERT C. WEISSELBERG

JOSEPH G. COWLEY

Drawings by Al Ross

McGRAW-HILL BOOK COMPANY
new york   st. louis   san francisco   london
sydney   toronto   mexico   panama

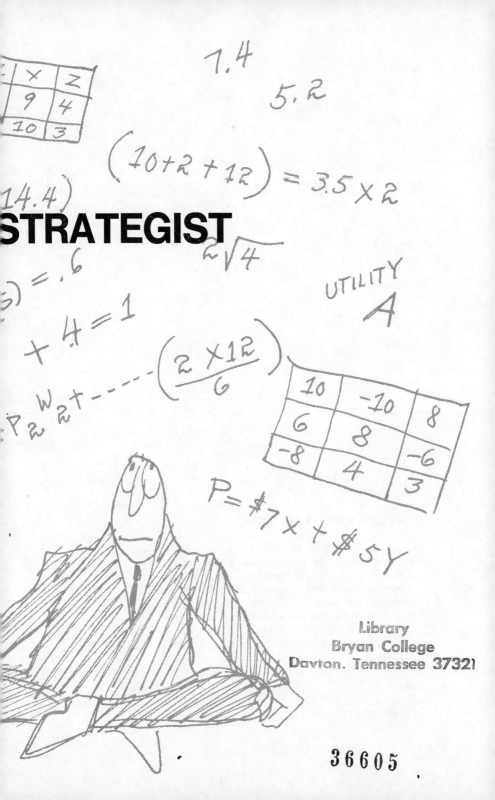

STRATEGIST

7.4

5.2

$(10 + 2 + 12) = 3.5 \times 2$

14.4)

$\approx \sqrt{4}$

) = .6

UTILITY

A

+ .4 = 1

$\left(\dfrac{2 \times 12}{6} \right)$

$P_2 W_2 + \text{-----}$

10	-10	8
6	8	8
-8	4	-6
		3

$P = \$7X + \$5Y$

X	Z
9	4
10	3

THE EXECUTIVE STRATEGIST

Library of Congress Catalog Card Number: 69-14493

69095

1234567890 VBVB 754321069

This book is affectionately dedicated to our wives, Margaret Weisselberg and Ruth Cowley, for their long-suffering patience during its writing.

A WORD IN ADVANCE . . .

On the need for an executive decision strategy

In the world of nature, the effect of a poor decision is swift and sure. The rabbit pursued by a hound takes the wrong turn only once. As Oliver Wendell Holmes, Jr., the Supreme Court Justice, once observed: "The judgment of nature on error is death."

In international affairs the cost of error can be high in money and human suffering.

In the business world, poor decisions mean loss of competitive advantage, diminution of market, and dwindling profits. They can also mean loss of jobs and (eventually) the decline of business empires.

It is the executive who must make most of the major decisions, and the measure of his worth lies in the quantity and quality of the decisions he is able to make. But increasingly today, such decisions are the product of groups.

The more complex the problem, the more people are required to define it, to gather the facts and analyze them, to seek solutions and test them, and to develop the solution that seems most likely to satisfy the decision criteria.

Management's increasing reliance on computers, scientific techniques, and other decision-making tools makes it natural for the executive to turn to specialists for help—to the management consultants, the systems engineers, the operations analysts, and others with scientific training.

It is the function of these specialists to help the executive develop decision strategies for various operational problems. Yet when a problem is diagnosed in mathematical terms, when a crosshatch of scientific disciplines is used, when the situation is represented by a mathematical or symbolic model, there is often a breakdown in communications. There is a gap between the scientist and the executive, a difference of terminology, objectives, and approach.

The aim of this book is to help bridge that gap by giving you some insight into how the scientific approach (whether it's called *scientific decision-making, operations research, management science,* or *quantitative analysis,* etc.) can help you make better decisions. It will introduce you to some of the basic decision-making techniques being used to solve operational problems today. It will tell you briefly and simply what they are and show you how and when they can be applied. And it will give you a familiarity with the scientist's terminology, if only as self-protection against those who resort to jargon.

In short, this is not a technical text but an easy-to-read guide to scientific decision-making, written by authors who are themselves management-oriented rather than technical specialists, for the executive who is assumed to have little or no specialized training in the subject. The knowledge available here should make you better able to deal with the problems that confront you, to know which are susceptible to scientific analysis, to know when to call in an expert, and to be better able to define your wants and better able to judge and utilize the solutions proposed. This, we believe, is a substantive part of what it means to be an effective *executive strategist.*

Robert C. Weisselberg
Joseph G. Cowley

ACKNOWLEDGMENTS

The authors would like to acknowledge their debt and express their appreciation to the following people: Edgar A. Grunwald, editor-in-chief of *Purchasing Week,* who first suggested this book and thus started the whole thing; our colleagues at EBS Management Consultants and the Research Institute of America for permitting us to bounce some of these ideas off them; Emma Green, Muriel Bayer, Doris Horvath, Sheila Bernard, Leonie Nowitz, Lynne Williams, and Penny Denton for their help in typing portions of the manuscript; Raymond M. Ferris for technical advice and a review of the manuscript; Thomas J. Johnson for his encouragement; but most of all the hundreds of specialists and operational executives whose ideas we have borrowed and tried to explain. Whatever limitations and errors of fact and interpretation the book may evidence are, of course, strictly our own.

R.C.W.
J.G.C.

ACKNOWLEDGEMENTS

CONTENTS

THE EXECUTIVE STRATEGIST

1

BY WAY OF INTRODUCTION . . .

The case of the golden apple

The popular impression of the successful executive is of one "who is not afraid to make decisions." This myth includes the idea that there is only one magic moment of choice. But the time dimension is missing: the decision process starts long before and continues long after the instant of choice.

Decision-making is seldom a simple matter of "yes, we go" or "no, we don't," nor does it necessarily take place at a single moment. Most problems in business and government take time to solve and have implications for various parts of the organization. If, for example, an industrial firm is considering acquiring a smaller company to round out its product line, many questions would enter into the decision:

- What is the fundamental *purpose* of making such an acquisition? (Although "expanding the product line" is the stated reason, the underlying goal is more likely to be company growth or increased net profit.)

- Is the proposed acquisition the best way to achieve that basic goal?
- What are the various ways such an acquisition could be made? What manpower, facilities, and money would be required for each alternative? What organization is needed?
- What would be the impact of each alternative on present operations of the company?
- Which alternative is best?
- What is a reasonable schedule for carrying out the decision?
- How can progress be measured in the task of absorbing the acquired firm? Has the basic purpose been accomplished?

The choice that appeared to be a simple, straightforward one (Should we buy Company X?) turns out to require answers to a series of subsidiary questions. This will not come as a surprise to today's executive, who practices an increasingly complex art, decision-making, in an increasingly complex environment—the interacting worlds of industry, government, and society. The executive is caught up in these complexities. The more involved the decision process becomes, the more of his time is demanded. And as the world about him grows more complex, the more critical each decision becomes. Because the stakes are high, he can't afford the luxury of a poor decision.

CONCENTRATE, QUANTIFY, DELEGATE, AND LEGISLATE

What can the executive do to relieve these pressures? Essentially, four things: *concentrate, quantify, delegate,* and *legislate.* By selecting problems whose solutions offer the greatest payoffs, he can concentrate his time and effort most effectively. He can construct models of his decision situations and obtain quantitative measures of the consequences of alternative choices. He can delegate much of the work of building and testing these models to knowledgeable specialists. And by formulating basic policies, he can legislate much of his decision-making, so that each procedural decision does not have to be made *de novo*. Not that these are new approaches—Jethro, an early consultant, advised his son-in-law, Moses, along these lines:

> Listen to me; I'll give you counsel. Teach your people ordinances and laws. Show them the way to go and the work they must do. And pick out men who can be rulers of thousands, hundreds, fifties, and tens. Let *them* judge the people, bringing only great questions to you. If you do this (and God command you do so), you'll be able to endure, and your people will live in peace.*

To do these things the executive must know a good deal about the business of decision-making: enough to make a selection among problems, enough to recognize problem patterns where quantitative techniques may be applied, and enough to describe the problem to the appropriate specialist.

A case history drawn from the war between the Greek city-states and Troy (in what is now Turkey) illustrates the problem of human fallibility—that of making a snap decision without measuring the odds or calling in the experts.

YOU HAVE WON SECOND PRIZE IN A BEAUTY CONTEST. (COLLECT $10.)

In Greek mythology, the story is told about how Eris, the Goddess of Discord, was miffed at being left out of a wedding reception. She tossed a golden apple marked "For the fairest" to the goddesses attending the banquet.

In the scramble for the golden apple, Hera, Aphrodite, and Athena asked Zeus who was the fairest. Wisely, the Father of the Gods declined to pass judgment. He referred them to Paris, a Trojan prince with an eye for beauty.

Each of the three contestants tried to bribe Paris: Hera offered him power and riches. Athena said she would get him wisdom and

---

* Exodus, chap. 18.

victory in war. Aphrodite promised him the most beautiful woman in the world.

Paris, who was young and hot-blooded, picked Aphrodite, the Goddess of Love. But Hera and Athena had little taste for ending up out of the money. Angry, the goddesses threatened trouble for Paris.

Nevertheless, Aphrodite made good her pre-election promise. She introduced Paris to Helen, a classic Grecian beauty. Unfortunately, Helen was already married to Menelaus, King of Sparta. But this didn't stop Paris. He kidnaped Helen and took her home to Troy, where his father was king.

Menelaus turned to his fellow Greek potentates for help. The Greeks mounted a land-and-sea attack across the Dardanelles. Helen was the girl with "the face that launched a thousand ships."

After a ten-year siege, Troy was finally taken by a trick. The Greeks hid soldiers in a hollow wooden horse left outside the city gates as a "peace offering." After the wooden horse was brought inside the city, the concealed soldiers opened up the gates of the city to the waiting invaders.

The snap decision that Paris made in giving the apple to Aphrodite cost him his own life, the sacking of the city, and the massacre of his fellow-citizens.

Moral of the story: When there's only one prize in a beauty contest, the second prize is bound to be jealousy. Look with ill favor on the snap judgment, particularly if it means choosing the best looker among three jealous goddesses.

**GO DIRECTLY TO JAIL. (DO NOT
PASS GO, DO NOT COLLECT $200.)**

Where did Paris go wrong? Might a decision-strategy have led to a better choice in this unfortunate situation? Let's see.

He was certainly selecting a problem with strong potential pay-offs: love, power, and wisdom. However, the *net* effect of choosing only one of these could be detrimental in the long run. It might have paid Paris to measure the alternatives quantitatively.

At first glance, the odds were 2:1 against Paris. No matter which goddess he picked as winner, he was sure to line up the other two ladies against him. He might, therefore, have considered which two goddesses could make the least trouble for him.

The odds were not really 2:1, because the alternatives were un-equal. Things might have been better if Paris had picked Hera. As the wife of Zeus and chief goddess, she might have been able to calm down the other two. And if Athena had been picked, her arts as Goddess of Wisdom and War might have helped Paris against the others.

Statistically speaking, Aphrodite was probably the worst possible choice. Her chief talent, as Goddess of Love, would be of little avail to Paris if Hera and Athena turned on him (as they did).

With the odds stacked against him in any possible choice, Paris could only lose. Best strategy? Possibly, call in a friend to advise him. Any good consultant would have warned him against making a choice. Perhaps he would have been well advised to toss the hot apple back to Zeus.

**YOU HAVE BEEN ELECTED
CHAIRMAN OF THE BOARD.
(PAY $50 TO EACH PLAYER.)**

The trouble with Paris was, he didn't understand the game he was playing. In effect, he had been put in a position comparable to the executive's, where his choice would affect the lives and fortunes of many people, including his own. He didn't realize that the alternatives offered (love, war, and wisdom) were symbolic of philosophies that might guide his life—hardly a matter for snap judgment.

Is today's executive more likely to recognize the critical situation that requires careful consideration? He is, if he knows the basic rules of the decision-making game. The essentials of decision-making are quite simple and fairly well known. But perhaps a few paragraphs in this introduction are appropriate. Permeating the whole book of rules is the concept that decision-making is . . .

A PURPOSIVE ACTIVITY

The organization has its reasons for being (profit for its owners, service to the public, etc.). Within the organization, there are various groups, with functions and goals that vary widely. Thus it is perfectly natural for one organization to encompass a great diversity of objectives, overlapping and conflicting. A company wants to pay a good dividend this year to attract investors; it also needs to expand sales for long-term growth and profit. Opening new branch offices will reduce funds available for dividends, yet should lead to expanded business.

The typical dilemma for the executive lies in selecting from all the available objectives the appropriate mix to apply to the problem at hand. The decision can then be made in the light of the immediate goals. To know how good your decision has been requires measuring it in terms of these objectives (that is, to what extent has implementing the decision meant achieving the goals that have been set?).

If we start with this basic premise (that each decision must serve a purpose, the successful decision being one that accomplishes its purpose), then it is easy to understand . . .

HOW WE DECIDE

The decision machinery is turned on early, even before the problem is defined, and it ends long after the solution has been chosen and put to work. Here, in brief, are the steps in the decision-making process:

- *Recognition.* A decision situation comes about when there is a problem to solve or an opportunity to explore. *Problems* are often obvious when there is conflict or failure in performance. *Opportunities* are less apparent and need to be actively pursued. It was President John F. Kennedy's choice "to reach out and select key issues, to initiate deliberations, to anticipate crises" rather than to decide "only what cannot be decided below, or only what others present." *

- *Definition.* Some objective is being violated, or is being inadequately met. Before the problem can be solved or the opportunity pursued, the governing objective must be defined. The problem or opportunity can then be stated, including the criteria for a successful solution.

- *Analysis.* The problem is broken down into its component parts so that it can be studied. Facts are gathered. Critical factors are identified.

- *Synthesis.* This step, which may begin before analysis ends, includes creating, building, manipulating, and weighing of models of possible solutions. Creativity frequently demands a period of inactivity, a turning-away from the details, giving the subconscious a chance to come up with fresh ideas. A solution may be tried out in real life; or a model may be constructed so that various solutions can be manipulated, tested, measured, and compared with the objective for the decision.

- *Choice.* This is the moment of decision (yet it may seem anticlimactic if the long process of synthesis has brought forth one alternative that is obviously better than any other).

- *Implementation.* Putting the decision to work includes determining the timing for implementation, assigning responsibility, and communication (e.g., announcing a change in policy or procedure that is to be implemented).

- *Follow-up.* Frequently overlooked, a post-decision audit helps insure that the implementation is proceeding as planned. Even more important is the measurement of results to see how successful the decision was: did it achieve its defined objectives?

* Theodore C. Sorensen, "Decision-Making in the White House," Columbia University Press, New York, 1963.

HOW TO PASS THE BUCK

The complex decision is generally a shared experience. But not all phases of decision-making can be shared, any more than love-making can be assigned to a committee. The executive must be deeply involved in the recognition and definition of decision situations, particularly so that he can select those problems and opportunities that are most worthy of pursuing. If he can delegate the analysis and synthesis to specialists, so much the better, but the responsibility for choice is his. At the time of choice, he steps back into the act. By weighing and testing in his own mind the alternative solutions (and possibly modifying them) he adds his own knowledge of the enterprise and its needs. By this act of self-involvement he invests his choice with an actual commitment to the course of action and involves himself in seeing that his decision is carried out.

The task of analysis and synthesis—of investigating the problems and opportunities and building real or model solutions—has gotten to be quite a specialized business. Much of this problem-solving work is therefore best delegated to specialists, either internal staff or outside professionals. Their use extends the range and depth of the executive's decision-making capability.

Assigning analytical tasks to specific individuals or groups is a primary responsibility, one which distinguishes today's executive from his predecessors. With the act of choosing the appropriate "thinking resource" he has delegated some of his decision-making authority and has identified the group that is to carry the ball. When you consider that decision-making is generally the last function to be shared with subordinates, it is obvious that the executive process has reached comparative maturity.

The distinguishing feature of operations research, systems analysis, organization planning, and other such disciplines is that responsibility is now designated for *analyzing* operations, not just for *performing* them. Other people are becoming involved in the decision-making process. And this is a most important step forward.

TO WHOM THE BUCK IS PASSED

Does the executive need to become a sort of traffic manager for problems, in order to delegate them? Unfortunately, the answer is often *yes*, because specialists tend to view most problems in the light of their own experience. Just because they are specialists, they are apt to view your act of delegation as meaning that you want their discipline applied (and no other). The same limitation applies to specialized consulting firms, to educators, and to other professionals with great depth in a particular body of knowledge. They all tend to take the same limited approach.

A selection among the analytical disciplines, therefore, calls for some knowledge of the models, techniques, and methods that may be applied. The various disciplines are distinguished mostly by the kinds of models that are constructed, by the techniques for developing solutions, and (to a lesser degree) by the methods of analysis. For example:

- *Systems analysis* uses graphic models (such as flow charts and organization charts) and written models (procedures, practices, etc.). This discipline frequently uses the computer, both as a model with which to simulate operations and as a tool for implementing the systems that have been designed.
- *Engineering* uses many different models to describe physical operations and processes, energy, materials, and structures. Among these are iconic models (such as construction models) that resemble the real thing, analog models that stand for processes and systems, and symbolic models (such as mathematical formulas) that are easy to manipulate. Industrial engineering, which is concerned with people and their performance in production and distribution activities, uses many of the same models as systems analysis. So does systems engineering, which is concerned with the control of operations and processes.
- *Accounting* uses numerical models (mostly dollars), both to record past transactions and to look to the future. Accounting is recognized primarily by its working tools: journal entries that re-

sult in a monetary picture of the organization at a given moment in time (the balance sheet) or over a period of time (statements of earnings and application of funds).

▪ *Economics* also utilizes numerical models, expressed in dollars, units of resources (materials, manpower, etc.), or units of production, and displayed in written or graphic form. These models seldom portray the immediate operating problems of the enterprise, but rather the way it is affected by regional, national, and international economic conditions.

▪ *Organization planning* and *industrial psychology* are two disciplines dealing with people within the organization and with their relationships; the models used are primarily verbal, written, or graphic.

▪ *Marketing research* and *public relations* are concerned with relationships that the organization maintains with people outside. One uses statistical and other models to measure the market and predict customer action; the other uses verbal and written communications to create a favorable image (a conceptual model) in the public mind.

▪ *Statistics* is both a discipline and a tool. As a discipline, it is concerned with mathematical models, such as samples representing a much larger "universe." Its purpose is to measure operations and to find meanings and trends in these measurements. Because it is observational, statistics differs from operations research and other disciplines, which use it as a tool to improve operations.

▪ *Operations research* is best known by its extensive use of mathematical models and techniques (linear programming, queuing theory, probability theory, simulation, etc.), which serve one main purpose: to maximize the effectiveness of operations. Perhaps even more important for the executive are its approach and method of analysis—operations research uses interdisciplinary teams to avoid overspecialization, and it adheres to the scientific method in approaching decision situations.

When the executive has a complex problem that does not readily seem to fall into an identifiable specialty, he would do well to discuss it with a management consultant or other professionals knowledgeable in various disciplines. He might also turn to the management sciences, such as operations research and information management, where teams of professionals with widely varying backgrounds are able to range beyond a narrow field of specialization.

SCIENTIFIC DECISION–MAKING: SUBJECT OF THE BOOK

Most of the disciplines that have been mentioned (accounting, engineering, etc.) are familiar to the executive. The newer management sciences, being less familiar, are the principal focus of the book, which is a discussion of scientific decision-making from the executive's point of view.

Many of the chapters deal with those kinds of problems that may be recognized and solved, a foundation for the executive's overall decision strategy. Some chapters explain quantitative techniques that may be applied. A checklist of "strategy briefs" that will help you identify the problems that can be solved with management science techniques is given at the end of the book, beginning on page 225.

With this introduction to the subject, it is appropriate to consider some of the newer trends in management decision-making.

2

FAREWELL
TO THE SNAP DECISION . . .

New trends in management decision-making

Decision-making is so vital to the executive function, whatever the business or field, that the executive who ignores the advances taking place today does so at his own peril. In business, in government, in education, in hospitals, in the military—indeed, in any large organization and in many smaller ones—the same changes are occurring. There are fewer, more critical decisions being made at a higher level; many subsidiary decisions are being made automatically; and, with the help of decision strategies and computerized solutions, the decision process as a whole is being transformed from an intuitive skill to a science.

A pattern that is becoming typical is this: the top executive (or team) makes a policy decision to investigate a new approach (the feasibility of automating order fulfillment, say). Specialists are called in (possibly systems, computer, or operational analysts) to design a recommended program to meet the criteria set up by various executives of the firm. If the program (with any new equipment it entails) is accepted and installed, many decisions once made by a supervisor or manager (details of when and what to ship, when and what to reorder, for example) are now specified by the system via decision strategies.

The advent of the computer, however, has only emphasized a trend already in progress: the shift away from many individual, intuitive decisions to programmed, formula choices. Every memorandum or procedure that describes how work shall be done or decisions made is a formula or program, a strategic policy. Decisions that flow from that formula, that are more or less repetitive and routine, are "programmed decisions." Computers are particularly adept at this kind of decision-making.

Despite this, the determination of objectives, the selection of strategies, and the responsibility for results, as well as broad policy decisions and the establishment of basic guidelines for the systems and the programs, will always remain the responsibility of the executive. However, because of the complexity of the problems faced and the high cost of error, the executive will come to rely more and more on specialists thoroughly grounded in scientific method and trained in the use of the newest equipment and techniques. The approach, the equipment, and the techniques all fit together. One of them would not be possible without the other two.

While this book is *not* about computers—their fantastic computational speeds, their ability to store and instantly retrieve vast amounts of data, and their capacity to solve problems quickly and accurately are essential to the scientific decision-making techniques with which this book *is* concerned. Therefore, it will be well, as we go on to discuss various decision-making strategies spawned by the management science approach, to keep them in mind as the tools that make the techniques feasible.

BETTER DECISIONS THROUGH
MANAGEMENT SCIENCE

The scientific approach to decision-making is primarily the application of mathematical and other techniques borrowed from various technical disciplines to the solution of operational problems faced by business or other large organizations. "Operations research," one name for this approach, abbreviated "OR," came to flower after its successful use by the military in Great Britain and the United States during World War II, and since then has found increasing acceptance by industry—particularly in such easily identifiable tools as linear programming and queuing theory. But its widespread acceptance has had to wait upon the development of more and better computers and more and better-trained personnel to apply it to business problems.

The primary task of OR practitioners has been to develop quantitative bases for management decisions. A mathematical model, itself, is a set of formulas representing relevant features of the system, or organization, or operation, under study. By developing such a model, we can evaluate how effectively the system will operate as a function of the variables, at least one of which is subject to control. The great advantage of a model is facility of use; it may be seen and understood more readily and manipulated more easily than the real thing—and usually at considerably less cost.

Your company's balance sheet, for example, is a model of your firm's financial status that can be seen and understood and projected to a much greater extent than the real but complex situation it portrays. A procedure is another model (though nonmathematical) —in this case, of how work is performed—expressed graphically (by means of a flow chart, etc.) or in words. If a chart is used, it can demonstrate visually how operations are related, who reports to whom, etc. But most of the models used in operations research with which we shall be concerned are algebraic in nature.

For example, here is a formula, or model, that fits most of the problems we shall be considering:

$$E = f(C_i, U_j)$$

This is just a shorthand way of saying that the effectiveness of any system (E) is a function (f) of the variables subject to control (C_i) and the variables not subject to control (U_j). The subscript letters (i, j) simply identify each of the variables.

Operations research utilizes this, and similar models, to analyze and recommend solutions to various "operational" problems. These, by definition, are problems involving the operations of a business or organization which normally can't be brought into the laboratory for solution (for example, the deployment of a fleet of trucks between a limited number of warehouses and many customers).

You could, of course, try to solve such problems by trial and error (the normal procedure before the advent of management science). But how would you know when you had arrived at an optimal solution? Or you might try to create a physical (nonmathematical) model of the problem. For example, in the case of the trucks, you could utilize a map, counters for the trucks, a rate schedule, records of supply and demand, etc. But, again, how would you know when you had arrived at an optimal solution?

The beauty of most of the management science techniques involving mathematics and computers is that they can often provide optimal solutions, or approximately optimal solutions, through the exploration of large numbers of alternative solutions until the point is reached where further search is not worthwhile (if possible). Your job, as executive strategist, is to recognize—and pose—problems that might be solved by these techniques.

CATEGORIES OF PROBLEMS
AMENABLE TO THE SCIENTIFIC
APPROACH

Although we are still finding new uses for the scientific approach to management problems, most such problems, it has been found, fall into one of several categories. Chief among these are:

Inventory problems. These are problems involving idle resources (usually materials, but sometimes men, money, machines, etc.) which must be maintained to meet an anticipated demand. With a few exceptions, virtually *all* businesses *must* maintain inventories of one kind or another if they are to remain profitable operations. The question is, what is the most profitable inventory level to maintain? If inventories are too high, you will pay excessive costs in terms of capital tied up, warehousing, insurance, possible obsolescence of stored items, etc. If inventories are too low, you will pay excessive costs in terms of lost sales, quantity discounts not realized, storage space not utilized, the necessity for more frequent ordering, etc. The answer, obviously, lies in determining the inventory level at which the total of both kinds of costs is minimized.

Allocation problems. These are problems that arise out of the need to allocate most effectively available resources to a number of possible uses or demands. These problems can take a number of forms. The *assignment* of men to machines might be one of these problems. The trucking problem just mentioned is a *transportation* problem that falls into this category. The determination of which warehouses are to serve which customers is a *distribution* problem of this nature. Even the best location of a facility (plant, warehouse, distributor, etc.) in terms of customer demand is an allocation problem. The question is, how can you best match the sources of supply available to you to known or anticipated demands? The answer involves weighing a complex (usually) set of variables with the help (usually) of a computer.

Queuing problems. These are problems stemming from a waiting-line (or bottleneck) situation that is fixed (i.e., is a necessary part of the operation). Like inventory problems, waiting-line situations involve two sets of costs that must be balanced against each other: in queues, the costs of delay versus the costs of service. If we minimize delay, we maximize service; and vice versa. It is a problem that is found most often, perhaps, in the operation of a service facility. For example, how many machine repairmen should a factory maintain? If it employs too few, the men may be kept busy but the costs of delay in repairing production equipment may be exceedingly costly. If too many, the costs of delay may go down but the men may be idle (unused) a high percentage of the time. A service facility *almost always* involves idleness (waste). The question is, How much can be most economically tolerated?

Sequencing, or control, problems. These problems, essentially, are concerned with planning-scheduling, or controlling resources (work, time, money, etc.), in order to achieve the desired results most effectively. They are unlike queuing problems, where the objective usually is to eliminate waiting lines (i.e., there is little economic necessity for them—in fact, eliminating delays is often our sole concern). The primary emphasis in sequencing or control problems is on reaching a certain goal within the shortest time possible consistent with maximum effectiveness and minimum cost. For example, the problem might be how to best utilize your resources (men, money, machines, materials, etc.) to hit the market as soon as possible with a new product. In a very large sense, this comes down to determining who is to do what, when, and in what order. Basically the question is, When the jobs to be done outnumber the facilities (men and machines) available to do them, what sequence of assignments, or control, will produce an optimum solution?

Routing problems. These are problems requiring the selection of the best routes or paths for the flow of work, men, trucks, material, etc. While routing problems may sometimes bear a superficial resemblance to sequencing problems, the important factors are topographical, rather than chronological. The question is, What routes will be most efficient (usually in terms of costs)?

Search problems. These are problems involving the most efficient procedure for finding something—a ship on the ocean, an error in a business process, the one right opportunity among many (Who are the prospects for a product your company might manufacture?). Obviously there are many factors to be considered in a search problem: cost, time, value of the "find," the search method, etc. The question is, How can the search be most efficiently conducted?

Information problems. These are problems that relate to the structuring and provision of data. For example: What information is needed for effective decisions (*flow-of-information problems*)? Or, how can facts be filed so that they can be found when needed (*information retrieval*)? What would happen to sales, operations, or finances if a given course of action were adopted (*corporate model problems*)? What changes in the economy might affect potential markets for goods and services (*problems of input-output analysis*)? In other words: What information is needed to support executive planning and control activities, and how best can it be organized and used?

Replacement problems. These are problems arising from the fact that men, machines, and other tools and facilities wear out by virtue of age, use, or obsolescence and need to be replaced. The question is, When is it most economical to replace such items? Do we wait until they fail, or do we replace them before they fail (absolutely)? The problem is complicated by the fact that not all items of the same make or nature fail at the same rate, and that some items fail suddenly and completely without warning (lightbulbs, for example), while others gradually deteriorate (machines, for example) with increasing inefficiency (often). If we wait until absolute failure before replacing an item, the loss in efficiency over a period of time and the loss of production when the failure occurs may be excessive. Should we replace items (like lightbulbs) as a group, or is it more economical to deal with failure in each individual case?

Competitive problems. These are problems involved in maintaining a position vis-à-vis the competition, usually in the market place. The problem may be to break into a new market, to compete effectively, to "win" a fair share of the market, or to maintain a superior position. The important uncontrolled variables in such a situation are the "other people"—and it is frequently difficult, if not impossible, to place a proper valuation on such variables. That wouldn't be so bad, except that *what* they do determines the relative success or failure of our own approach to a solution. The question is, What strategy is it best to adopt when a full knowledge of competitive strategies is impossible? This is a problem found in most games—though the results here are seldom win-or-lose, all-or-nothing, complete success or complete failure, as they are in games. But businesses *do* fail!

THE NATURE OF MANAGEMENT
SCIENCE PROBLEMS

This categorization of management science problems does *not* mean that all operations problems fall neatly into one category or the other. Some problems may be difficult to classify, some may appear to fit one classification yet actually belong in another, and some problems are complex enough to be broken down into several categories. However, the breakdown can be useful in helping *you* spot problems amenable to the scientific approach, and in helping the analyst determine the technique and model required.

Such problems are not always manifest. You might, for example, be quite satisfied with your distribution setup—but is it the best that can be achieved? You won't know unless you ask the question and utilize scientific techniques to determine an optimum solution. On the other hand, you might *think* you have a problem when one doesn't actually exist. For example, you might walk by the tool crib, see two attendants reading comics, decide that your firm is wasting money, and yank one of them out. But this could be a costly error. The scientific approach can tell you how much idle time is most economical.

If the problems that can be solved by management science are not necessarily obvious, then the good executive strategist is one who remains alert to them, who asks whether the operations for which he is responsible are the best that can be achieved, and who is not satisfied until those operations are functioning at, or close to, optimum. This means not only knowing where to look for such problems, or potential problems, but recognizing them potentially or actually when you come across them. There are certain characteristics that distinguish such problems.

First, since management science is concerned primarily with operations, we are likely to be dealing with open-ended systems and open-ended solutions. That is, the problem is ongoing. We don't come up with *final* solutions. For example, after we determine the best inventory level to maintain, a change in price could alter the level. The real value of a scientific solution is that it produces a model of that particular inventory, so that it is easy to feed in the new value and come out with the new solution. The real work has gone into recognizing and defining the problem, digging up the facts about the system, quantifying the values, and creating the model.

A second characteristic of management science problems is that you *must* be able to quantify the variables involved (i.e., assign numbers to them). This does not immediately disqualify problems involving subjective factors—it simply makes their solution more difficult. In fact, the ultimate decision in any case (despite the determination of an optimum solution) is often a qualitative (i.e., subjective) one.

Finally, and most important of all, a management science problem involves a system that can be duplicated in the form of a model (usually mathematical). This is essential—though sometimes difficult to determine. In some cases, the analyst may have to do considerable digging before deciding that a model adequate to a solution can, or cannot, be created. But in most cases, if *you* have been knowledgeable in calling him in, he will be able to come up with a model and a technique.

SOME WIDELY USED MANAGEMENT SCIENCE TECHNIQUES

Management science techniques, as we have indicated, derive from a wide variety of disciplines and usually have names that indicate those particular disciplines, that are given them by their inventors, or that indicate the types of problems to which they are chiefly applied.

However, three things about them should be emphasized: First, since this is still a developing science, new variations and refinements of existing techniques are constantly being developed. Second, complex problems are likely to utilize more than one technique for their solution. And third, none of the models involved can ever fully reflect *all* the complexities of any particular operational situation. In short, it is not reasonable to expect always to find a perfect "fit" between problem and technique, to expect "pat" answers, or to expect that you as an executive can suspend your judgment or abdicate responsibility for the solution.

If the definitions that follow seem somewhat obscure, this will clear up (we hope) as we delve more deeply into the subject in later chapters. Here, then, are some of the most widely used techniques and their applications:

Mathematical programming. This includes techniques based on mathematical concepts taken from the calculus, higher algebra, and geometry and utilizing (in most cases) matrixes (an array of numbers) for the manipulation of variables. These techniques include linear programming (the easiest to understand and the only one we shall take up in any detail), nonlinear programming, and dynamic programming. Linear programming concerns itself with problems that can be expressed by linear equations and inequalities, while nonlinear programming deals with nonlinear relationships. Dynamic programming involves solving a series of related problems one step at a time because the solution to one problem affects the answer to the next. Mathematical programming is used mostly to solve allocation problems, where a number of limited resources must be used to satisfy a number of competing demands, and is best done in most cases with the help of a computer. In short, it's an optimization process, under a series of constraints.

Queuing, or waiting-line theory. This consists of techniques that apply to problems involving fixed waiting lines of units (men, machines, tools, etc.) that need servicing. You may already have noticed the similarity between queuing problems and inventory problems. Both problems stem from the factor of uneven demand (if demand were even, there would be no problem), and the solution lies in determining how much idleness (of men, machines, or materials) is most economical to build into the system. The techniques, and the models involved, to solve servicing problems of this nature must take into account *four* factors: (1) the total of the units that may require servicing, called the *customer population;* (2) the *waiting line* itself, whose most economical length we want to determine; (3) the *facility* available to do the servicing (a tool crib, maintenance men, barbers, etc.); and (4) what is called the *service discipline,* the rule by which each unit is selected for service (first-come, first-served, etc.).

Statistical analysis and probability theory. These include overlapping techniques and concepts taken from the field of statistics which are useful (if not essential) in dealing with, or extracting the meaning from, large masses of data. These statistical tools are fundamental in applying most of the other management science techniques. They involve basic measures like *range, mean, standard deviation, percentiles,* etc., which are useful in spotting essential data, monitoring trends, assessing results, and establishing cause-and-effect relationships. Probability theory is essential, of course, in establishing the statistical likelihood of any particular event or events occurring.

Simulation, or Monte Carlo. This is a technique that involves the generation of random numbers to represent chance factors as input to a model. In using the term, we usually mean a more complicated re-creation of the system than a simple formula. In fact, such systems are usually too complicated for mathematical analysis or formulation. And in the strict sense, simulation is the manipulation of the relevant data to suggest a better *approach* to the problem rather than to produce any final solution. Such simulation is usually performed on a computer. Simulations with which you are probably familiar are business "games" played with the help of a computer.

Replacement, failure, or reliability theory. These are techniques designed to help you deal with the timing and selection of replacements for machines, components, materials (even men), etc., that eventually fail, either slowly (through deterioration or obsolescence) or suddenly. Taking the failure rate, or probability of failure with time, into consideration, these techniques help you to relate the costs of failure with preventive maintenance costs, replacement costs, etc. Failure costs, of course, include loss of production and possible loss of sales. There is a variety of models available for testing and solving these kinds of problems.

We have given you only a brief look at a few of the major management science techniques. In the rest of this book, we shall take a closer look at these and other techniques—and their application to the problems you face.

3

THE STANDARD
GAMBLE AND OTHER PLOYS . . .

Some of the concepts and terminology
of basic decision theory

Before we begin examining specific management science techniques, it will be helpful to look at some of the basic theories underlying decision-making.

Basic decision theory is called just that because it is basic to most of the special problem situations we shall be considering. It is theory that is independent of any particular situation or problem calling for a decision. To a very large extent, what we are going to do is to define some of our terms and rearrange some of our thinking. But this is essential if we are, first, to understand the operations analyst and, second, to understand with any degree of precision (i.e., scientifically) the operational problems and their solutions that confront us.

An executive faced with a problem usually has a number of alternative choices leading to a solution. In scientific lingo, these alternatives are known as *strategies*, hence your role as an executive strategist. To determine which strategy is best, we need an *objective function* (goal), and some kind of decision *criteria* (measures of success). Problems always involve two kinds of variables (factors, elements, events, etc.)—those that are subject to your control and those that are not.

The uncontrollable variables are sometimes referred to as *states of nature* because the "world" imposes them upon us or *random* variables (occurring by chance). A *sequence of events* with a certain probability associated with each is known as a *stochastic* process. Choosing the *optimum* (best) strategy means manipulating the controllable variables in light of the uncontrollable, or random, variables so as to achieve our objective.

THE PAYOFF MATRIX: A VERY USEFUL TOOL

One of the most useful of all the management science tools is the payoff matrix, particularly in the solution of competitive problems (involving game theory) and allocation problems. A payoff matrix is simply a representation of the basic formula on page 15 in the form of a grid, or chart. In other words, it is a more graphic model. The formula, as you recall, says that the effectiveness of any system (or the *expected value* of any solution) is a function of the variables subject to control and those not subject to control. Effectiveness (E), of course, is the payoff, and by substituting P (payoff) for E we say the same thing.

To illustrate the payoff matrix, let's start with a very simple, non-business situation: betting on a horse race. You are at the track, you have $2 to bet, and a race is coming up. The variable subject to your control (the *fixed* variable) is the disposition of that $2. You can bet or not bet. If you bet, you can bet on any particular horse, win, place, or show. The variable *not* subject to control (the *random* variable) is the outcome of the race. The horse you bet on may win, place, show, or finish out of the money. What should you do?

If your objective is to return from the track with as much money as possible, you have a problem. Although it does not fit any standard

Uncontrollable variables

	U₁	U₂	U₃	U₄
C₁	P_{11}	P_{12}	P_{13}	P_{14}
C₂	P_{21}	P_{22}	P_{23}	P_{24}
C₃	P_{31}	P_{32}	P_{33}	P_{34}
C₄	P_{41}	P_{42}	P_{43}	P_{44}

Controllable variables

FIG. 3.1.   **Payoff Matrix**

technique, the problem will be clearer if we express it in the form of a matrix. If we let the rows represent the controllable variable (C_1, C_2, etc.) and the columns represent the uncontrollable variable (U_1, U_2, etc.), then we can look for the payoff (P_{11}, P_{12}, P_{21}, P_{22}, etc.) where row and column conjoin.

States of nature

	Win	Place	Show	Lose
Win	10	-2	-2	-2
Place	5	5	-2	-2
Show	3	3	3	-2
No bet	0	0	0	0

Strategies

FIG. 3.2   Horse-betting Problem in Matrix Form

The matrix above in Figure 3.1 is a generalized representation of an OR problem as expressed by the formula, $E = f(C_i, U_j)$. Obviously, the subscripts (the subset numbers) indicate the rows and the columns (i = the rows; j = the columns), so that P_{23}, for example, represents the payoff indicated in the square at the conjunction of the second row and the third column. The matrix makes it quite clear that the payoff is a function of (depends upon) *both* the variables. If, for example, we select (or establish) C_2 as our variable (which we can do, since we control it), and U_3 is (or turns out to be) the uncontrollable variable that exists, the result will be as indicated at P_{23}.

That the matrix is a model becomes very apparent if you imagine it to represent the layout of an office, with each of the squares standing for a desk. As a chart, you might use it, for example, to look up who's sitting at the desk in the third row, fourth column (location 34, in other words), and find that it's Paul. Thought of in this way, it's also easier, perhaps, to understand how such information (any problem information) can be stored in a computer and retrieved. What happens if we select C_3 as our controllable variable and U_2 is the uncontrollable variable that exists? Press button 32 (this is oversimplified, of course) and find out.

The matrix shown in Figure 3.2 represents our little horse-betting problem in matrix form. Of course, it does not represent all eight horses, but only one of them. Also, it does not take into consideration the horse's chances (the probability of each of the states of nature occurring), the state of your bankroll (an important consideration, as you will find out), or your intuitive "feeling" about the horse and the race (a consideration which can be quantified and which is not as "unscientific" as you might think). But the matrix is useful, nevertheless. It tells us what the payoff will be (in dollars, assuming a bet of $2) if we select one of the strategies available to us (bet win, place, or show, or don't bet) and one of the four states of nature possible occurs (the horse runs first, second, or third or loses).

IT'S ELEMENTARY:
THE ALGEBRAIC MODEL

We are about to devote only a page or two to mathematics, even though mathematics is one of the most essential (if not the most essential) of the disciplines underlying the management sciences. Even so, no adequate comprehension of the scientific approach is possible without the recognition of at least two elementary algebraic models. One of these (the equation) you have already been introduced to. The other, which is also necessary to describe many problems, is the inequality (non-equation). Let's look at them both in terms of a very simple problem.

Imagine that you own a factory with one machine in it that can be worked 40 hours a week (beyond that, overtime makes it prohibitive). On this machine you can produce two products: A and/or B, but not both at the same time. The machine can produce 200 units of A per hour, at a profit of $7 per 100 units, or 300 units of B per hour, at a profit of $5 per 100 units. Your problem is: How much of each would you produce each week to maximize profits? While the answer (in this case) may be obvious, let's set the problem up as an algebraic model utilizing the equation and the inequality.

The basic equation we need is one that expresses the efficiency of our system—which in this case is to be measured by profit. If we let x equal 100 units of A, and y equal 100 units of B, then the profit we make on this machine will be determined by the following equation: $P = \$7x + \$5y$. This states mathematically what we have already said in plain English: that we shall make $7 profit on every 100 units of A we produce, and $5 profit on every 100 units of B. That this is not a complete model of the problem is obvious. If it were, we would produce an infinite number of A's and/or an infinite number of B's for infinite profit.

In actual fact, the problem involves certain restrictions or restraints—mainly, that the machine can work for only 40 hours a week, and that it can produce *either* 200 units of A per hour *or* 300 units of B. These are production limitations, but the problem could just as well involve limitations in demand, manpower, supplies, etc. But let's keep it simple. To complete the model, what we need is a *constraint* equation (or inequality, as the case may be) to express the production limitations. Quite simply, this is: $\frac{1}{2}x + \frac{1}{3}y \leq 40$.

In plain English, this says that the value of x cannot exceed 80 (200 units of A per hour times 40 hours), the value of y cannot exceed 120 (300 units of B per hour times 40 hours), and the total values on the left side of the equation (or inequality) must be equal to or less than ($\leq$) the value on the right. This is easy to check out. You assign a value of 80 to x if y is 0, and assign a value of 120 to y if x is 0, but any combination of the two cannot exceed the value of 40 on the right. There is another constraint that might be taken for granted but which is frequently expressed. And this is simply that $x \geqq 0$ and $y \geqq 0$. In other words, both x and y must be

at least equal to 0 (i.e., they have no negative value). The complete model, then, is

$$P = \$7x + \$5y$$
$$\tfrac{1}{2}x + \tfrac{1}{3}y \leqq 40$$
$$x \geqq 0, y \geqq 0$$

Any solution, therefore, will be determined by, and must satisfy, this equation and three inequalities.

THE STANDARD GAMBLE: MEASURING THE UNMEASURABLE

So far, the problems we have mentioned have had variables that were more or less easily quantified. But many, if not most, problems involve subjective factors that you may not want (or it may not be wise) to ignore. For example, OR may indicate that you need only two clerks to service a facility—but you "hate" to keep people waiting; OR may tell you where to locate a plant—but you prefer a location "with a little more class"; OR may tell you to drop the distributor in Minneapolis—but "Harry is a good friend of yours," and you feel you "owe" him something.

In a sense, these are simple problems. Management science can tell you how much a third clerk will cost you, how much the prestigious location will cost you, and how much it will cost you to keep "good old Harry" as a distributor. All you have to do, then, is to decide "whether or not it is worth it to you."

This kind of executive judgment, of course, will always be called for. But there is another class of problem, where the subjective factor is not so easily quantified and where you cannot always be assured of making the right choice. For example, here is an illustration from the Research Institute of America: "There are two movie theaters in your town and you want to make the late show at either one or the other. It is Saturday night and you know the theaters will be crowded. You much prefer to see the picture at theater A, but there's a 30% chance you won't get in. If you go to theater B, there's a 10% chance you won't get in. The theaters are on opposite sides of the town, so if you go to one you definitely won't be able to get in the other. If you don't go to see a movie, your evening will be ruined. Which theater should you go to?" *

Similar problems are not at all uncommon in the business situation. For example, you have the problem of selecting either A or B as your assistant. On the basis of tests, experience, and other qualifications, A would appear to have a 90 percent chance of succeeding in the position, while B's chances are only 80 percent. But you would prefer working with B. Which executive do you choose for promotion? Fortunately, a rather ingenious approach to this type of problem was worked out by two scientists, John von Neumann and Oskar Morgenstern, in a book called "Theory of Games and Economic Behavior." † They called it the "standard gamble," and it involves something called . . .

THE BERNOULLIAN CONCEPT OF UTILITY

The concept of utility is simply the recognition of the fact that the value of anything depends upon its utility to the person who

* Research Institute of America, "The Standard Gamble," *Tomorrow,* October, 1965.

† Princeton University Press, Princeton, N.J., 1947.

has it or wants it. If we offer a pomegranate to the first ten people who write us a letter on the evils of OR, you are less likely to respond if (1) you dislike pomegranates, or (2) you already have so many pomegranates you don't know what to do with them. In short, pomegranates have very little "utility" to you.

Daniel Bernoulli, an eighteenth-century scientist, first wrote about this in relation to money. He recognized the fact that money is not an entirely *objective* measure of value, because the value of money will depend on its *utility* to the person who has it or wants it. As a general rule, the value of money to us will vary inversely in proportion to the amount we already have. (For example, a $10 raise will mean more to the person earning $100 a week than it will to the person earning $1,000.)

Bernoulli suggested using the logarithm of the amount involved as an approximation of its utility; but since the subjective variable may *not* be money (and even if it is, the subjective evaluation may be determined by factors other than quantity possessed), the standard gamble is a more useful means of determining its utility. The standard gamble, to be specific, will help us assign numbers to subjective values so that they reflect their relative value to *you*. You will then be in a position to make a more rational choice of alternative solutions to a problem, using standard OR techniques if necessary.

For example, let's go back to that problem of selecting either A or B as an assistant on page 31. The subjective variable in this case is the preference for B; the risk is that either A or B might fail (*F*). Since failure in either case has the same disastrous consequences (loss of production, excessive work on your part, the cost of finding another assistant, etc.), there are really only three outcomes to this problem: the success of A, the success of B, and the failure of either. Let's therefore label these outcomes *A*, *B*, and *F*.

We want to make a rational choice between *A* and *B* in a situation involving a variable risk that might result in *F* (failure). We have a problem, of course, only because we prefer B, who has a higher risk of failure. The decision is whether our preference for B is so great that it is worth the extra risk involved in hiring him. We know the extra risk (i.e., it has been quantified). To make a rational decision, following standard operations research techniques, all we have to do is to quantify our preference and measure the utility of the outcomes.

As a first step toward solution, the standard gamble technique asks us to arbitrarily assign two numbers to the outcomes with the highest and lowest utility. (It actually doesn't make much difference which two numbers we use, but it is conventional to use 1 and 0.) Since successful B is the outcome with the highest utility, we shall assign a value of 1 to B; and since F is the outcome with the lowest utility, we shall assign a value of 0 to F. To make a rational choice, all we have to do is determine the utility of A. And this, we know, lies somewhere between 1 and 0.

THE SEARCH FOR THE UTILITY OF A

To find the utility of A, von Neumann and Morgenstern suggest that we offer ourselves a series of choices between getting our second-best outcome (successful A) with certainty, and gambling on getting either the most-desired outcome (successful B) or the least-desired outcome (F) when the probabilities of getting B and F are known and are complements of one another. In this case, your choice will always be between A for sure and a lottery where your chance of getting B is p (probability) and your chance of getting F will therefore always be $1 - p$.

By varying the value of p from 1 to 0, you will eventually arrive at a point where it is difficult to make up your mind between A for sure and the lottery between B and F. When you arrive at this point, you will be faced with what the authors call the "standard gamble." And at this point p will have the value you should assign to A as the measure of its utility.

For example, in the case we have been considering, if we assign a value of 1 to p, the chance of our getting B in the lottery is 100 percent, and the chance of F occurring is $1 - p$, or 0. Therefore we would take a chance on the lottery, since it's a sure thing, rather than choose A with certainty. But suppose p has a value of 0.90 (there's a 90 percent chance of getting B in the lottery and a 10 percent chance of F), what would your choice be? A for sure or the lottery? Still choose the lottery? Then continue to lower the value of p until we reach that point where the choice between A for sure and the lottery seems even-steven.

Let's say that we reach the standard gamble (we can't make up our mind between A for sure and the lottery) when p has an assigned value of 0.70. This value then becomes the measure of the utility of A. The problem is then a matter of determining the *expected value* of both A and B, using the measure of utility you have established, and selecting the possibility with the highest expected value.

The expected value is obtained by multiplying the utility of an outcome (the payoff measure) by the probability of its occurring. For example, the expected value of B is 1 (the measure of utility we assigned to it) multiplied by 0.80 (B's chances of success in the job), or 0.80. The expected value of A is 0.70 (the measure of utility we just determined by means of the standard gamble) multiplied by 0.90 (A's chances of success in the job), or 0.63. On this basis, the choice of B as your assistant is likely to be more satisfying to you than the choice of A.

MORE ON EXPECTED VALUE AND UTILITY

The above is a particular application of expected value, but basically it's just a fancy way of saying that over the long haul the payoff for a certain event will *average* such-and-such a value. Probability theory, which we'll get into a few chapters from now, helps us determine that average so that we can apply it to a particular event. If we know the probabilities of all the possible outcomes or payoffs for a particular event, then the expected value of that event is the sum of each of the payoffs times its probability. In mathematical form,

$$\text{Expected value} = p_1 W_1 + p_2 W_2 + \cdots + p_i W_i + \cdots$$
$$+ p_n W_n = \sum_{i=1}^{i=n} p_i W_i$$

where p equals the probability, W equals the payoff or numerical outcome, and $\sum$ is the *sigma*, or summation sign, for a number of payoffs and their probabilities, ranging from 1 to n.

For example, if you invest \$1 in a lottery where the probability of loss is 0.99 and the probabilities of winning one of three prizes are: \$100, $p - 0.001$, \$50, $p - 0.004$, and \$25, $p - 0.005$, what is the expected value of the event (the drawing)? According to the formula, it is the sum of each of the four outcomes, or payoffs, one of which happens to be negative (i.e., involves a loss). Or,

$$\text{Expected value} = 0.990(-\$1) + 0.001(\$100) + 0.004(\$50)$$
$$+ 0.005(\$25)$$
$$= \$.425 - \$.990 = -\$.565$$

In other words, over the long haul you can expect to lose an average of approximately 56½ cents every time you play the lottery.

Would any rational person invest money in this lottery? The answer is *no*—or possibly *yes*. Definitely *no* if the dollar has an equivalent utility regardless of the quantity of them involved. It may be, however, that a single dollar invested in this way once a week has little utility ("After all, what can I do with a dollar? It's the equivalent of a couple of packs of cigarettes, which I can easily do without.") in that the pain of loss is offset to some extent by the pleasure of gambling, while winning one of the prizes would provide you with the pleasure of a night on the town, or a brief vacation, which you would otherwise not normally be able to enjoy. Thus, the utility of the single dollar is less than 1, while the utilities of the prizes are more than 25, or 50, or 100 times 1. This you would have to decide.

In general, the more money you possess, the less attractive this kind of investment will appear to you—not because the single dollar has greater utility to you, but because the prizes have less. The event (the drawing in the lottery) might even assume a negative expected value greater than that determined without utility as a factor. You would then either not invest, or would turn to investments with a greater expected value. For example, you might choose to invest \$1,000 in stock A with a 0.65 probability of returning 8 percent on your investment (or no return at all), or $1,000 in stock B with a 0.90 probability of returning 5 percent (or no return at all). The expected value of stock A's return is 0.65 × $80 = $52, while that of stock B is 0.90 × $50 = $45.

This does not mean that a rational person with a certain minimal affluence does *not* ever invest in a lottery. Most men, as a matter of fact, *do*—whenever they buy insurance, which is a lottery of sorts. Because of the varying utility of money, it may be rational for you to insure your lifetime income through life insurance, say, and your property through fire insurance, and just as rational for the insurance company to issue the insurance. The concept of expected utility can give you some idea of whether to insure or not.

For example, let's say that you own jewelry worth $20,000 (which is most, if not all, of your assets), and that the probability of its being lost or stolen in the year ahead is 0.01. Does it pay you to buy insurance, and how much should you be willing to spend in annual premiums? Should an insurer with assets of $100,000 assume the risk for you, and how much should he charge? If we follow Bernoulli's suggestion and use the logarithms of the amounts involved as a measure of utility, we can come up with answers.

First of all, the cost of insuring your jewels against loss or theft, whether you self-insure by *not* taking out insurance or the insurance company carries the risk, will be $20,000 × 0.01 = $200 (the *average* loss per year as determined by probability). From a rational viewpoint, if utility were not a factor, it would not be logical for you to pay more than $200 a year for the insurance. But the insurer has administrative, sales, and other costs to add to the risk, and he cannot profitably insure your assets for less than $300. Why, then, do insurance companies exist and do people take out insurance?

The answer lies in the concept of utility. Following Bernoulli's suggestion, the utility of $20,000 is the logarithm of that amount, or 4.3010, times 0.99 (the probability of retaining the amount if you self-insure), which is 4.2580 (the utility of approximately $18,100, the amount for which 4.2580 is the logarithm). On the other hand, if you pay for a year's insurance, cashing in some of the jewelry to do so, you will retain $20,000 − $300 = $19,700, with a utility (the logarithm of this amount times 1.0) of 4.2945. Thus, your expected utility if you insure is higher by $1,600 ($19,700 — $18,100). It, therefore, would pay you to insure at this premium.

What about the small insurer with assets of only $100,000? Does it pay him to assume the risk? If he doesn't insure you, he will retain all of his $100,000 with a utility of 5 (the logarithm of this amount) times a probability of 1. But if he *does* insure you, he will have $100,300 with a utility of approximately 5.0013 times a probability of 0.99, equal to 4.951287, and $80,300 (assuming a loss of $20,000) with a utility of 4.9047 times a probability of 0.01, equal to 0.049047. The total expected utility of the insurer if he assumes the risk is therefore 4.951287 + 0.049047 = 5.000334, which is the logarithm for an approximate value of $100,070—a gain in utility, and therefore some justification for assuming the risk.

4

THE FOUR
BASIC DECISION SITUATIONS . . .

The conditions under which we decide

In general, a decision must be made under one of four conditions, and these conditions will determine the technique most applicable. It's useful, therefore, in devising a strategy to solve a problem, to be able to determine first the conditions under which the decision will have to be made. This will provide you with a generous clue to the type of problem you face and the type of approach you will need to solve it. The four basic decision situations are: (1) decision-making under certainty, (2) decision-making under risk, (3) decision-making under conflict, and (4) decision-making under uncertainty. Let's examine each of them in turn.

DECISION–MAKING UNDER CERTAINTY

Many (perhaps most) decisions fall into this category, especially if we include the many more or less "trivial" problems that beset us

from day to day. For example, we know for sure that some unwelcome "friends" are planning to drop in on us Sunday, so we "decide" to be out (but if there's only a 50 percent chance that they
will drop in and, while we don't want to receive them, we also

don't want to go out, that's a horse, or a problem, of a different
color). The distinguishing feature of this kind of situation (in OR
terminology) is that the state of nature is known. In the example
just given, the state of nature is the unwelcome friends showing up
at our front door. That's uncontrollable. The controllable variable
is our own position: in or out. Figure 4.1 shows the problem in
matrix form.

State of nature

Strategies		Friends
	In	Pain
	Out	Pleasure

FIG. 4.1.   Matrix for "Friends" Problem

Of course, this is a very simple problem involving only two rows
(controllable variables) and one column (uncontrollable state of
nature), and the payoffs are absolute. The decision also is perfectly
clear, assuming that the decision criterion is hedonistic—to seek

pleasure and avoid pain (if you're a masochist, the decision is still clear). But suppose that you don't want to go out (i.e., it will give you pain)? This is still decision-making under certainty, and will remain so as long as the state of nature (your friends showing up at the front door) remains 100 percent certain. However, you may have to make a fairly agonizing decision (and science will not be of much help) as to which choice or strategy will have the biggest payoff (i.e., give you the least pain).

While we have used an example from personal life, many business decisions are also made under conditions of certainty. For example, you may have your choice of five machines on which to produce product X (i.e., have your choice of five strategies), where the fixed cost (state of nature) is known. If you imagine this as a matrix (as above), you will find that you have five rows and (again) one column, with the payoffs (in terms of cost) indicated in each box. If your object is to minimize costs, you simply run your finger down the column and select the machine opposite the box where the least cost is indicated.

The distinguishing characteristic of decision-making under certainty, since the state of nature is known, is that there is only *one* state of nature—hence there will be only one column when you express such problems in the form of a matrix. But problems this simple do not require OR, or a matrix, for their solution. OR becomes necessary, however, when the problem is a *compound* of similarly simple problems and the solution of each is related to the solution of each of the others. For example, if we take that little production problem and add four more products, we have a fairly simple allocation problem (Figure 4.2).

The first column expresses the original problem, and solving it is just a matter of going down the column headed "X" and selecting the machine (in this case M4) that will produce that product at least cost. But we've added four additional products, which compound the problem. For example, product B can also be produced at the least cost ($3) on machine 4. Which product do we therefore assign to M4, assuming that our overall objective is to minimize *total* costs? This problem is still simple enough to solve by visual examination and a little pencil work.

But suppose we add a few constraints. Suppose, for example, that the costs indicated are for 100 units of each of the different products, that each of the machines has varying production rates for each of the products, that the demand for each of the products varies, and that if any of the machines is worked more than 40

States of nature
(costs of producing products)

		X	Y	Z	A	B
	M1	12	9	3	5	8
	M2	9	10	11	4	7
Strategies (choice of machines)	M3	8	13	12	9	6
	M4	6	15	8	4	3
	M5	14	10	11	9	7

FIG. 4.2.   Allocation Problem in Matrix Form

hours a week, production costs on that particular machine increase by 50 percent for the overtime hours. Our problem now is to supply maximum demand at minimum cost. What products, and in what quantities, do you assign to each of the machines? This, as you are well aware, is a more typical problem. And an optimum solution can be greatly facilitated by the use of scientific techniques.

DECISION–MAKING UNDER RISK

We move on now to problems that (theoretically at least) are more difficult—and therefore perhaps more interesting. This does *not* mean that they are necessarily more difficult to solve. Problems of the variety discussed above, for example, can involve so many strategies and states of nature that it is literally impossible to evaluate all the payoffs—even with the help of all the computers in existence. Problems requiring a decision under conditions of risk, on the other hand, may be easier to solve in some instances but are more challenging and interesting.

Take the case of the unwanted friends mentioned on page 40. The "horse or problem of a different color" we referred to is where there is a 50 percent chance that the friends will *not* show up at our front door on Sunday. We still have two choices (strategies) open to us (to remain in the house or to go out), but now there are *two* states of nature possible (friends on our doorstep or no friends on our doorstep). In cases like this, there could be limitless numbers of states of nature, but the distinguishing characteristic is that the probability of each of the states of nature occurring is known with a reasonable degree of certainty. Knowing the risk, which strategy do we select? For example, take a look at Figure 4.3.

States of nature

		Friends	No friends
Strategies	In	0.50 Pain	0.50 Pleasure
	Out	0.50 Pleasure	0.50 Pain

FIG. 4.3. "Friends" Problem Complicated by Risk

This, obviously, is a little more difficult problem (in theory) than the similar problem where it is known for certain that the friends are going to call. The matrix makes it clear that there are now *four* possible payoffs (in terms of pleasure or pain) instead of two, while the percentage figure in the upper right-hand corner of each payoff square indicates the probability of that particular state of nature occurring if we select that particular strategy.

The first step in solving a problem like this on a scientific basis is to quantify the payoff measures (pleasure-pain). This can be done by using the standard gamble technique (see page 30) to determine the utility of the pleasure-pain on a scale (-10 to $+10$, 1 to 10, 0 to 1, etc.) running from extreme pain to extreme pleasure.

Next, multiply the measure of utility by the probability to determine the expected value of each of the payoffs. Then select that strategy opposite the row containing the payoff with the highest expected value.

But this problem is oversimplified to such an extent that it undoubtedly prompts you to ask a number of questions. First of all, if our decision criterion is the maximization of pleasure, isn't it obvious that we need concern ourselves with only two possibilities (payoffs in squares X_{12} and X_{21})? And since there is a fifty-fifty chance of either of these states of nature occurring, can't we ignore the probability of either of them occurring and simply decide whether it will give us more pleasure to be out if it is certain our friends *will* call, or in if it is certain that they *won't* call? And isn't this simply decision-making under certainty?

The answer to all three questions, of course, is *yes* . . . but. Decision-making under risk is rarely this simple. For example, suppose that it will give us a pain in the neck to be out in either case and our only pleasure is in staying home. Suppose that there's an 80 percent chance that our friends will call. Suppose that our matrix, with utility values (of pleasure) as extreme as those indicated (on a scale of 0 to 10), looks like Figure 4.4.

States of nature

		Friends	No friends
Strategies	In	0.80 ⌐ 0	0.20 ⌐ 10
	Out	0.80 ⌐ 2	0.20 ⌐ 1

FIG. 4.4. "Friends" Problem with
Utility Values

Our expected values (utility times probability) for each of the squares in this case are: $X_{11} = 0$, $X_{12} = 2$, $X_{21} = 1.6$, and $X_{22} = 0.2$. If our objective is to maximize pleasure, then we would elect to stay at home and take our chances. If our objective is to minimize pain, then our utility measures would simply be the converse of these (i.e., $X_{11} = 10$, $X_{12} = 0$, $X_{21} = 8$, $X_{22} = 9$), and we would still elect to remain at home, since the payoff with the *lowest* expected value (i.e., pain) is indicated in square X_{12}. However, it may be that the payoff for X_{11} is intolerable, in which case we have no choice but to be out. This is to say that we would not rationally make any choice where the payoff is utterly intolerable (e.g., bankruptcy, death, etc.), unless the probability of the state of nature occurring is insignificant.

DECISION–MAKING UNDER CONFLICT

Most executive decisions fall into one of the two categories already discussed. However, one of the essential conditions of life, and of business life in particular, is conflict. Organizations, like organisms, exist among competitive constraints, and their growth, survival, or decline is determined to a greater or less extent (but usually to a much greater extent than most people realize) by the nature of the competition and the changes effected by that competition and, above all, by the nature of the environment of which they are a part.

This competition is apt to be keenest among those organisms or organizations most alike (i.e., which are competing for the same limited means of sustenance or survival, such as a particular market, in the case of a business). So in a larger, though very real, sense, *all* decisions come into this category, since all decisions made on behalf of an individual or organization ultimately affect the survival of that individual or organization (in a qualitative, if not quantitative, sense).

For example, the determination of inventory levels will affect profits, and ultimately your position vis-à-vis the competition within an industry. But if you think of the competition at all in making a decision of this nature, it usually enters the model as a restraint (e.g., if the competition offers immediate delivery, then you may have to maintain an inventory adequate to provide the same service). What we are now concerning ourselves with are problems where the moves of a rational opponent are of *major* concern to us in making our decision—where, indeed, the possible moves of a competitor are entered in the model as states of nature, and where the payoff is determined by the strategy we select and the state of nature that prevails at the time the payoff occurs.

Obviously, we are entering an area where the problems, in general, are a little stickier and the outcomes resulting from decisions will be less readily predictable. In some respects, decision-making under conflict is less "scientific," leaving more room for the executive's intuitive "feel" for a situation, for imaginative solutions, and for informed judgment to come into play. In part, this is due to the fact that our opponents do not always act rationally, that the information necessary for a scientific decision is often impossible to obtain, and that theory and decision-making techniques in this area are still imperfect.

Marketing, war, and games immediately spring to mind when one thinks of situations involving conflict, but there are many others (two or more men bucking for the same promotion, for example, is one) where the decisions must be made under conditions of conflict. Basically, this is a situation where what one person (or firm) gains is at the expense of another, and vice versa. This is a complicated subject, and many of the techniques were first worked out on the basis of games (hence the name, *game theory*). While we shall deal with this subject in more detail in a later chapter, let's look at a simple illustration involving a "two-person zero-sum game."

Take those unpleasant "friends" of yours again (nasty chaps, aren't they?). They're really malevolent, and their only pleasure in life is making you suffer. In fact, their pleasure is in direct proportion to your pain—and vice versa. Now, this Sunday afternoon you have only three places you can go (you can stay home, visit Harry, or visit Bob), and the friends know it. What is more, they know Harry and Bob, and can visit *them* if they wish. As far as you are concerned, staying home and having your friends call on you would be much the worst situation, because they would not only have the chance to bore you utterly, but they would also drink up your Scotch and clean out your refrigerator.

You don't want to go out, and the happiest condition would be to stay home and *not* have your friends call. If you went to Harry's it might not be so bad; he serves good Scotch, he has a beautiful wife, and they would make the visit of the friends less painful if they show up. Bob, however, doesn't serve Scotch and he has a shrewish wife, but it would still be better to be there with your friends than at your own home. In short, we can make up a payoff matrix for this problem showing the payoffs for you or your friends in terms of pleasure-pain. For example, Figure 4.5 shows the problem from your point of view, with the payoffs expressed on a scale of −10 to +10. The minus figures, of course, indicate pain and the plus figures indicate pleasure.

"Friends"

		Your house	Harry's house	Bob's house
You	Your house	−10	8	10
	Harry's house	8	−6	6
	Bob's house	4	3	−8

FIG. 4.5   Matrix of Conflict Situation

Artificial though it may be, this situation has all the elements of the simplest "game." There are only two opponents and the conflict is complete (i.e., what you gain the opponent loses, and vice versa). However, it is not necessary that you and your opponent have the same number of strategies open to you; it would still be a two-person zero-sum game. Gin rummy is this kind of game; so is the problem where two employees are competing for the same promotion and only one of them can get it.

Obviously, the "games" become more complex the more opponents (or players) there are, the more strategies there are, and where the payoffs are not necessarily zero-sum (i.e., one opponent does not necessarily gain or lose entirely at the expense of the others). In real life, most "games" do not involve complete conflict of interest and are therefore *not* zero-sum. For example, in choosing advertising media, you may gain or lose vis-à-vis the competition (i.e., if his advertising is more effective than yours, he may take business away from you), but the sum of the effectiveness of the advertising that both of you buy may expand the *total* market and thus *increase* your business. However, more of this when we get to Chapter 14, "How to Tackle a Smart Opponent."

DECISION–MAKING UNDER UNCERTAINTY

The prime characteristic of problems that require you to make decisions under conditions of uncertainty is that the probability of any of the states of nature occurring is unknown. The "friends" problem, for example, falls into this category if we know nothing about their feelings (we don't even know that it gives them pleasure to give us pain), and we have no clue as to which house they are likely to visit—yours, Harry's, or Bob's. All we know is that they are going to call at one of those three places on Sunday afternoon, and their presence would pain us. In this case, they aren't an opponent, but a state of nature we wish to avoid.

Many important business decisions fall into this category: how much to invest in a particular research project when the payoffs are utterly unknown, whether or not to undertake a major plant expansion when the payoff will depend upon states of nature (war, economy, market, etc.) that will prevail ten years hence, whether to invest in the development of a product for which the demand cannot be predicted, etc. In short, our problem falls into this category if past experience provides no relevant data on which to base reasonably accurate predictions of the probability of the various states of nature that determine the payoff occurring. And the question is, How can we make *any* decision if we have no way of knowing what is going to happen?

Actually, it's questionable as to how scientific decisions made under these conditions will be. For example, there is considerable dispute as to how big a role subjectivity should play in problem-solving, particularly in setting up decision criteria. We've already seen, for example, that money is not necessarily an objective criterion, and that subjectivity plays a big part in determining its utility. This problem of objectivity-subjectivity becomes particularly acute in dealing with decision-making under uncertainty. When what is going to happen is unknown, then the selection of a strategy will be influenced greatly by the subjective feeling or attitude of the decision-maker. For example:

Faced with the "friends" problem on page 46, you may have a feeling that the worst is going to happen (i.e., that whatever choice you make, the friends are going to be there). Since you don't know what state of nature is going to occur, this assumption (that nature is malevolent) is as valid as any other. Your criterion then becomes one of pessimism, and your objective is to "maximize the minimum"—to select that stategy which assures the least loss. In this case, you would choose to go to Harry's house, where, if your friends show up, you will suffer the least pain.

On the other hand, you may be a complete optimist and assume that the best is going to happen (i.e., that, whatever your choice, your friends will *not* be there). Your criterion, then, is one of optimism, and your objective is to "maximize the maximum"—to select the strategy with the maximum payoff (in this case, to stay home). However, we are seldom 100 percent optimistic, and we can make a more rational decision if we introduce what is called a *coefficient of optimism*. In other words, *how* optimistic do we feel? This can be determined (as in the case of the standard gamble) by assuming a lottery between the maximum payoff and the minimum payoff (i.e., between the payoffs in squares X_{11} and X_{13} in the matrix in Figure 4.5).

If it were 100 percent certain that the friends were going to Bob's, we would elect to stay home. But suppose it's only 90 percent probable that they are going to Bob's, and 10 percent probable that they are coming to your house. Would you still elect to stay home? Keep juggling the figures, and eventually you'll reach a point (say, at 0.65 and 0.35) where you're not sure whether you'd stay home or not. These figures then become your coefficients. The next step is to apply these coefficients to the maximum and minimum payoffs for each of the strategies, add the results for the strategy together, and select that strategy with the biggest expected payoff. For example, in this case, as Figure 4.6 shows, our best strategy is strategy 2 (go to Harry's house).

Another interesting criterion is that of *regret*. Its objective is to minimize the regret we might feel if the wrong strategy is selected.

Strategy	Maximum payoff	Minimum payoff	Expected payoff
1	10	-10	10(0.65) + (-10)(0.35) = 3.0
2	8	-6	8(0.65) + (-6)(0.35) = 3.1
3	4	-8	4(0.65) + (-8)(0.35) = -0.2

FIG. 4.6. Expected Payoffs Using Coefficients of Optimism

And regret can be measured by the difference between the best that might have been and what actually occurred. For example, if we elect to stay home and the friends show up at our front door, our regret would be a combination of the happiness (8) that might have been ours if we had gone to Harry's, and the unhappiness (−10)

"Friends"

		Your house	Harry's house	Bob's house
You	Your house	18	0	0
	Harry's house	0	14	4
	Bob's house	4	5	18

FIG. 4.7. Regret Matrix for "Friends" Problem

that we actually received. On that basis, we can create a regret matrix for the entire problem, as in Figure 4.7. There, as you can see, the worst regret we could experience is 18 for strategy 1 and 18 for strategy 3. Applying the criterion of pessimism, we would therefore choose strategy 2—which is the best (14) of the worst.

Finally, we'd like to consider one further criterion, that of *rationality*. This criterion suggests that since we don't know which state of nature will occur, we should assume that the probability of each of them occurring is the same. Again, this is reasonably valid. Applied to the "friends" problem, our expected payoffs assume the values in Figure 4.8.

Strategy	Expected payoff
1	1/3 (-10 + 8 + 10) = 2.67
2	1/3 (8 + [-6] + 6) = 2.67
3	1/3 (4 + 3 + [-8]) = -0.33

FIG. 4.8. Expected Payoffs Using Criterion of Rationality

Our choice is a toss-up between strategies 1 and 2. However, this criterion, like the others, has serious limitations. We are, in other words, in an area where judgment is at a premium. This is what makes horse races and, in the final analysis, businesses. You, the decision-maker—the executive strategist—are at a premium. It is unlikely that a machine (or an OR analyst, for that matter) is ever likely to replace you. This should be kept in mind when we get to some of the practical applications of OR techniques. But first let's take a look at another specialized field that is important to scientific decision-making.

5

FACT OR
FICTION FROM FIGURES . . .

Statistical analysis as an aid
to decision-making

Imagine yourself with a group of figures (a collection of data), such as those in the table in Figure 5.1, which may be relevant to a decision you are about to make.

These figures could represent anything (sales of a certain product over the past 36 weeks, failure times in hours of a type of equip-

A.	102	154	253	267	423	069	235	175	184	392	271	259
B.	467	342	245	202	256	301	649	305	682	549	379	500
C.	409	375	653	468	598	974	743	608	549	705	830	552

FIG. 5.1. Collection of Statistical Data

ment, rejection rates for department B, etc.)—it doesn't matter. The point is, what do they mean? Unless you know, how can they help you make a rational decision? Well, the truth is, they don't mean much of anything unless they are analyzed. And that's where the science of statistical analysis comes in. It attempts to tell us what collections of numerical data like this mean, primarily by analyzing the relations that may exist between the numbers that compose the data, so that we can make rational decisions.

?	A	102	154	253	267	423
	B	467	342	245	202	256
	C	409	375	653	468	598

WHAT STATISTICS IS ALL ABOUT

In just compiling the above set of figures (or any other collection of numerical data you may gather together) you have taken your first step in statistical analysis. Others are: organizing and analyzing the data, evaluating conclusions, trying to spot cause-and-effect relationships, and keeping tabs on any trends or processes. Statistics offers you the means to achieve these objectives. For example, you may want to determine the *average* (or averages for each of the 12-month periods, if these are, say, monthly sales figures) and compare them, or to determine the *range* (in this case from a low of 069 to a high of 974, or range = 905), if such measures will help to make the data meaningful to you.

This chapter will simply explore in a little more depth some of the statistical terms and techniques that are so important to scientific decision-making. They are important, of course, because they help to quantify the information upon which management science decisions are based. But knowledge of statistics will heighten your appreciation of the need for accurate and reliable data in making *any* decision, and of the fact that statistics itself is not an absolute science and cannot be expected to make your decisions for you.

OBTAINING THE DATA YOU NEED FOR DECISION-MAKING

We rarely have *all* the data we need for making a decision, and in a very real sense statistics is the science of dealing with the unknown or of making inferences based on limited data. For example, the numbers in Figure 5.1 (representing information obtained over a period of time regarding sales, failure times, or rejection rates, etc.) may be *all* the data available at this time but are *not* all the data if they preclude previous or future information that *could* be included and might affect judgments or decisions based on the total group of data. The entire group of data that interests us is called the *population*. What we have in this (and in most other cases) is a *sample,* or part, of the population. Hopefully, it will be representative—that is, will tell us something about the population from which it is derived if we analyze it properly. Naturally, the larger the sample relative to the population, the more accurate any analysis of the sample is likely to be.

In some cases we work with a sample because the population figures are unobtainable. For example, we may not have kept adequate records (of machine downtimes, for instance) and the figures are forever lost. Or future facts, such as next month's sales, simply don't exist yet. Or the population figures may be physically impossible, or impractical, to obtain—such as the number of people alive in the world at this instant. But even if these restrictions did not exist, in many, if not most, cases we prefer to work with a sample because it is much more economical to do so and because the inferences drawn from the sample regarding the population (or *universe,* as it is also called) are likely to be accurate enough for our purposes.

In other words, as a general rule, the greater the sample, the greater the costs *and* the greater the precision of our analysis—

which means that in most decision situations the sample we decide to work with will represent a compromise between cost and accuracy.

ORGANIZING AND ANALYZING YOUR DATA

Once you have your data—a sample of the population you're interested in—the next step, obviously, is to take a look at the figures to see if you can make sense out of them as far as any decision you might have to make on the basis of them is concerned. This is where statistics can be of major value. It provides the tools for measuring the significance of the data we have gathered together. These tools, or measures, fall mainly into three general classifications: (1) *measures of goodness-of-fit*, (2) *measures of central value or tendency*, and (3) *measures of dispersion or variability*. Let's look at some of those most frequently encountered.

Of course, in gathering your data you may find that they have come somewhat organized or grouped for convenience in handling. For instance, if the data in Figure 5.1 are weekly sales data (number of units sold, say), then they have already been grouped by the week. And in this form they are perhaps more understandable than if they had been presented as a list of individual units sold (1, 1, 1, 1, 1, 1, etc.). Grouping the sales on a week-to-week basis, for example, gives you an opportunity to compare them and to make some kind of rough response to the question, "How am I doing?" which is an important question statistical analysis can help answer.

FREQUENCY DISTRIBUTION

This kind of grouping of the individual values, called "observations," that comprise our data is known as a *frequency distribution*. In this case we have listed the frequency with which an observation occurs during a certain period of time. But there are other ways of distributing the data. One of the most useful of these is what is known as an *observed*, or *empirical*, frequency distribution. For example, we may want to condense the data in Figure 5.1 still further by dividing it up into intervals of equal size and seeing how many of the observations fall into each of the intervals.

The number of observations that fall into each interval, or category, is known as the *observed frequency* of the events we are concerned with (whether weekly sales, failure times, or what have you), and from many of these intervals we can draw up a table called the *observed frequency distribution*, which may enable us to study the data more readily and draw from them more easily conclusions that may be meaningful to us. For example, if, using intervals of 100, we divide the data into 10 classes and count the number of observations that fall into each class, we shall get the observed frequency distribution table shown in Figure 5.2.

Sometimes it is useful to plot this kind of information on a graph so that we can "picture" our distribution. For example, if we create a bar graph, called a *histogram,* of the observed frequencies by class

Class interval units	Number of observations in each class	Observed frequency	Cumulative observed frequency
from to			
0 - 100	x	1	1
101 - 200	xxxx	4	5
201 - 300	xxxxxxxx	8	13
301 - 400	xxxxxx	6	19
401 - 500	xxxxx	5	24
501 - 600	xxxx	4	28
601 - 700	xxxx	4	32
701 - 800	xx	2	34
801 - 900	x	1	35
901 - 1000	x	1	36

FIG. 5.2. Observed Frequency Distribution of Statistical Data

intervals, and fit a smooth curve to it, we might get something like that shown in Figure 5.3 (which we shall ask you to contrast with the "normal" distribution curve in Figure 5.4). Frequency distribution histograms like these can be useful in helping us to understand and explain the data we are studying.

For example, we see at a glance that our distribution is *unimodal* (it peaks only once) and *asymmetrical* (it is slightly skewed or off-center). The normal distribution, by contrast, is not only unimodal

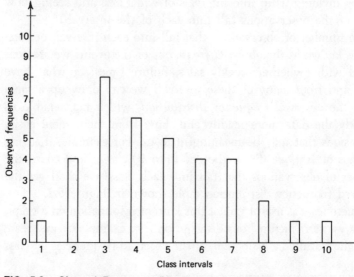

FIG. 5.3.   Skewed Frequency Distribution Histogram

but is symmetric. The number of modes and the symmetry are important in describing the distribution of data, since they will affect our measures of central value and variability if there is more than one mode or if the distribution curve is skewed. However, in dealing with a normal distribution, which exhibits a fairly symmetrical, bell-shaped curve, we can ignore mode and symmetry and use only measures of central value and variability to specify, or describe, it.

MEASURES OF CENTRAL VALUE OR TENDENCY

The histogram can be quite useful in helping us explain and illustrate some of the measures we are going to concern ourselves with. Measures of central value, for example, obviously have to do with the clustering of our data around some central value. One of the three most important of these, the *mode,* has already been described. It is indicated by the peaks in the distribution curve. A normal distribution curve, as we have seen, has only one mode, which represents the value that occurs most often. On a histogram it lies at the midpoint of the class interval that has the most frequencies of occurrence. In our example, the mode will be in the third class interval and would have a value somewhere between 250 and 251.

The other two measures of central value most commonly used are the *mean* and the *median*. The arithmetic mean, of course, is the average of our observations, or the sum of their values divided by the total number of observations. In a normal distribution, the mode, mean, and median will all be the same. But in our example the mean is 420, which is an indication of how skewed our distribution is, since the mean no longer represents the center of the distribution. Instead, the mean, weighted by the extreme values to the right, has shifted in that direction. This is illustrated in Figure 5.5.

The median, as you can see in the skewed-distribution illustration, is less affected by the extreme values than the mean, and it is therefore not pulled as far to the right. The median is simply that value which lies in the middle of all the values we are dealing with if they are ranked in order from lowest to highest. If two values lie

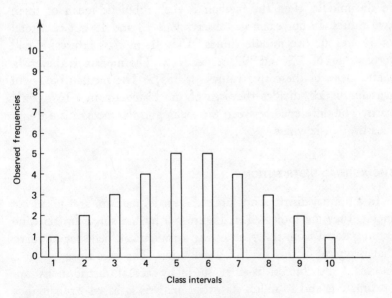

FIG. 5.4. **Normal Frequency Distribution Histogram**

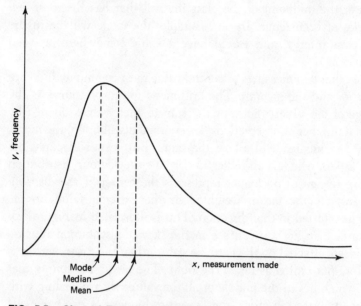

FIG. 5.5. Skewed Frequency Distribution

in the middle, then the median is the arithmetic mean of those two values. In our example, observations 18 and 19 out of a total of 36 are our two middle values. They lie in class interval 4 and have values of 379 and 392, respectively. The median is the arithmetic mean of these two values, or 385.5. The median, you will perhaps notice, divides the *area* of the histogram into two equal parts. The difference between the mean and the median is a rough measure of skewness.

THE NORMAL DISTRIBUTION

In a normal distribution, since the mode, median, and mean coincide, they are indicated in Figure 5.6 by the single broken line coming down from the peak of the symmetrical, bell-shaped curve that is typical of this kind of distribution. The nice thing about a "normal" distribution is that so many actual distributions approximate it and so much statistical analysis is based upon it that in many cases that is all we have to know about a sample or population to make a number of statements (or draw conclusions) relevant to the data.

For example, we know that in a normal distribution a certain percentage of the observations will lie with a high degree of certainty within certain specific intervals, known as *standard deviations*. A standard deviation is symbolized by the small Greek letter *sigma* (σ) when we are dealing with a population, or the small letter s when we are dealing with a sample. It represents a certain distance from the mean. The mean is symbolized by a *mu* (μ) for the population and an x-bar ($\bar{x}$) for the sample. Sometimes these distances from the mean, as indicated by standard deviations, are referred to as "sigma limits."

In any event, when the frequency of observations forms a normal distribution, on the average 68.27 percent of the observations will fall within one standard deviation from the mean (that is, from $\mu - \sigma$ to $\mu + \sigma$), 95.45 percent will fall within two standard deviations (from $\mu - 2\sigma$ to $\mu + 2\sigma$), 99.73 percent will fall within three standard deviations (from $\mu - 3\sigma$ to $\mu + 3\sigma$), etc. Such information can be looked up in tables. So probable is this pattern in a normal distribution that chance can be excluded as a factor in ac-

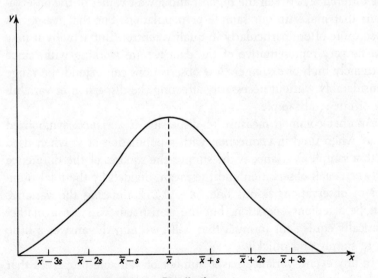

FIG. 5.6. Normal Frequency Distribution

counting for extreme deviations, which would encourage you to look for the reason for the exception. This is certainly helpful in monitoring events that should follow a normal distribution.

MEASURES OF DISPERSION
OR VARIABILITY

The standard deviation is a measure of dispersion, and in the opening pages of this chapter we mentioned another called *range*. Range is certainly the easiest measure to determine, being simply the difference between the highest and lowest values of the observations that make up our sample or population. For that reason it's used quite often, particularly in quality control. But actually it may not be very representative of the data we are working with, since extremely high or extremely low observations can extend the range considerably without necessarily affecting the dispersion or variability of our total sample.

Another common measure of dispersion is *variance*, symbolized as σ^2 when used in connection with a population or s^2 when used with a sample. Variance is the sum of the squares of the difference between each observation and the mean, divided by the total number of observations minus one $(n - 1)$. Estimating the variance can be a tedious operation, but the statistician will use a mathematically equivalent formula that will give him the answer a little more simply and quickly.

In any event, variance has a number of valuable properties that make it very useful, not the least of which is stability. Also, we need the variance to determine the standard deviation, which is the square root of the variance and which is the most important measure of dispersion we have. With measures like these, the statistician is in a position to evaluate the data before him and to draw conclusions from them that will be helpful to you in making decisions relevant to those data.

6

THE GENTLE ART
OF THE SMALL BITE . . .

Making sense out of samples with
statistical analysis

Any statement we make based on a statistical sample is in essence an educated guess, and therefore not necessarily valid—only probably valid. This probability, usually stated in percentages, is known as a *probability statement*. It is an expression of the *level of confidence* we have in the statement's being true or valid. This percent of confidence is also often referred to as the *confidence coefficient*.

Statistics are the characteristics of a sample (the characteristics of a population are called *parameters*). But it is easy to forget this sometimes—that statistics do not usually represent the population with 100 percent accuracy—and to act as if they did. In actual fact, it would be quite a coincidence if the statistics of a sample taken from a population were exactly the same as the parameters of that population. For example, the mean of a sample seldom is the same as the true mean value of the population. But in a normal distribution, we are 68.27 percent confident that an observation will fall within plus or minus one standard deviation of the sample mean.

This interval (from $\bar{x} - ts$ to $\bar{x} + ts$—where t is a coefficient dependent on sample size) is known as a *confidence interval*. The larger it is, of course, the more confident we can be that the statement will be true (i.e., that an observation will fall within those limits). Ideally, we should like the statistician to combine the smallest possible confidence interval with the highest possible level of confidence, particularly if any decisions based upon this statistical information are likely to have serious consequences. But this may turn out to be quite expensive.

In reality, we generally settle for a minimum level of confidence within a given confidence interval and ask the statistician to achieve this at minimal cost. The less serious the consequences of our decision (that is, the more risk we're willing to take), the wider the confidence interval and the lower the level of confidence we're willing to work with, since they cost less.

EVALUATING CONCLUSIONS AND TESTING HYPOTHESES

Determining the confidence coefficient that should be attached to any conclusion, statement, or hypothesis as an indication of its probable validity *is*, of course, an evaluation of that conclusion, statement, or hypothesis. This simply points up the highly probable nature of *any* statistical statement.*

Probability, then, is an important consideration in any evaluation of a statistical statement, in any consideration of the truth or falsity of a hypothesis, in any determination of the significance of

---

* It's easy enough to grasp this idea intellectually, but sometimes it's difficult to accept it in reality. For example, a statistician may tell you that there's only one chance in a thousand of failing if you try a certain venture. The tendency then is to act with certainty and, when the venture fails, to sneer, "Some statistician!" But, of course, the statistician did not tell you that the one event in a thousand would *not* occur—only that it was not too highly probable. But more of this when we get to the chapter on probability.

an event or occurrence, and in any comparison of related sets of data. However, it is *not* a function of the parameters of a population. For example, if our population consists of 100 people in a room, and by actual count we find that 46 percent of them are women, that is *not* a probability statement. On the other hand, if the group of 100 people is a random sample of some larger population, then we might hypothesize that the population is also 46 percent female. But how confident can we be (what is the confidence interval) that this is actually so?

Statisticians have a number of techniques for testing hypotheses, but most of these can get somewhat sticky. In general, their procedure, after adopting a hypothesis, is to select the appropriate *significance level* (probability level), determine the critical values (usually taken from established tables), and then, after doing the required computation, compare the computed value with the critical values and either accept or reject the hypothesis. Fortunately, there are also several simple rule-of-thumb tests that can be useful in testing a hypothesis.

THE SIGNIFICANCE OF SIGNIFICANCE

Significance is a term that is used often in statistics (indeed, we have already used the term several times ourselves and have indicated above that it might have something to do with probability), but what does it actually mean? It has to do with the probability of an event's occurring by chance.* An event, for example, may be said to be significant if the probability of its having occurred by chance is less than 1 in 20. This is smaller than the probability of getting four heads in a row if you were tossing a coin (you might try this several times if you want to get a real feeling for significance).

Of course, there are degrees of significance. An event that had only 1 chance in 100 of occurring might be highly significant, while

---

* The *null hypothesis,* which most statisticians provisionally adopt, assumes that an event (or variation) is *not* significant unless the probability of its having occurred by chance is very low.

an event that had only 1 chance in 10 of occurring would probably be considerably less significant. Keep in mind, however, that we are speaking of *statistical* significance, and when we say that something is significant, we really mean that it is *likely* to be significant, highly *likely* to be significant, or less *likely* to be significant. In other words, these are probability statements.

In dealing with a sample, the best we can do is to determine to what extent the difference is *likely* to be the result of random variations (i.e., exist in the sample alone and not in the population). In most cases, if there is less than a 5 percent chance of it existing in the sample alone and not in the population, we say that the difference is significant (i.e., we should make a decision as the result of it). Some of the questions that are most likely to concern us in determining significance are:

. . . whether the difference between the mean of our sample and a previous average, the mean of another sample, or a standard mean is significant;

. . . whether a variation in our set of figures is significant;

. . . whether our figures show a trend, and, if not, how much additional information we would need to determine whether or not there was a trend, etc.

Let's look now at . . .

SOME SIMPLE TESTS FOR DETERMINING SIGNIFICANCE

We've seen that one of the easiest measures of central tendency to obtain is the mean, but what does it mean (pardon the pun)? In itself, it's not of too much value. It assumes meaning in comparison with another mean, as indicated above. For example, if the average number of rejects per month in department A was 82 last year compared with 67 in department B, is this difference significant enough to possibly warrant investigation? The answer is *yes,* if the probability of the difference being due to chance is 5 percent or less. And the basic formula for determining significance is to subtract one sample value from the other and divide this difference by the standard error of the difference. But since there are several formulas for determining standard error,* depending upon the differences being tested, the type of sample value, and the size of the sample, this may get us more involved than we wish to be. In most cases, a rough test of significance will do.

For example, to return to the problem above, is the reject rate in department A significantly greater than that in department B? Using comparable values (e.g., percentages) from two independent series of observations taken over a 12-month period, we assume the mean of department B to be the standard. Let's say that the monthly rejects for department A were 74, 52, 58, 85, 144, 80, 75, 83, 85, 86, 93, and 79. There's no need to even compute the mean (this could be tedious and time-consuming if very many observations were involved); all we have to do is to count those observations with a value higher than our standard of 67 and those observations with a lower value, ignoring observations with exactly the same value.

In this case there are 10 observations with a higher value than 67 and 2 observations with less value. There is a significant difference between the mean of department A and our standard mean of 67 if the difference between the number of observations with a higher value and those with a lower value (assuming our test of significance is 1 in 20) is greater than twice the square root of the sum of those numbers. Since the difference $(10 - 2)$ is 8, and twice the square root of the sum $(10 + 2 = 12)$ is approximately $3.5 \times 2 = 7$, the difference is significant; and we'd be well advised to look into it.†

However, before doing so, we might well note that the value of one of the observations (144) seems to be out of line with the values of the other observations and wonder if the variation is significant. If it is, this could very well be throwing our mean off, since the variation may be a "stranger"—that is, not really belong to

* For example, there are formulas for determining the standard error of the mean, the standard error of the standard deviation, the standard error of the variance, the standard error of the coefficient of variations, the standard error of the median, etc.

† Keep in mind that statistics doesn't tell you *what* to do, only that you'd be justified on the basis of the available figures. It's quite possible that you might choose to ignore the difference for reasons of your own or choose to

the set of numbers. To find out if this is so, all we have to do is to subtract the lowest number in the set from the highest, first including the variation that is suspect, then excluding it. If the ratio between the two ranges exceeds 2:1, then the variation can be considered significant.

In this case, 144 (the highest number in the series *including* the suspected stranger) minus 52 is 92, while 93 (the highest number in the series *excluding* the suspected stranger) minus 52 is 41. The ratio between the two ranges does exceed 2:1; therefore the variation *is* significant. If we decide to check into it (since the chance of its having been due to chance is 1 in 20 or less), obviously one of the first things to investigate is whether the observation was recorded accurately. In this case, let's say it wasn't, and that it should have been 44 instead of 144. Our numbers now are: 74, 52, 58, 85, 44, 80, 75, 83, 85, 86, 93, and 79.

TESTING FOR A TREND

It would be easy, studying our set of numbers (notice, for example, that the reject rates for the last six months seem to run higher than those of the first six months), to convince ourselves that there is a definite trend upward in these figures and that we'd better do something about it before they get any higher. But before we rush into action, it might be nice to be a little more certain. Fortunately, there's a simple, rule-of-thumb test that will tell us whether the rise in the values of the observations is significant enough to indicate a trend.

All we have to do is divide the series of observations into three equal, or approximately equal, parts, and to compare each of the numbers in the third part with its equivalent number in the first part. To indicate a trend, the number by which the comparisons favorable to the third group exceed the first group must equal or exceed $2\sqrt{N}$, where N equals the total number of comparisons. In our case, our series divides evenly into three parts of four observations each. Three of the observations in group three exceed their counterparts in group one, while one number in group one exceeds its counterpart in group three, giving us $3 - 1 = 2$. Since this does not equal or exceed $2\sqrt{4}$, which is 4, the increase is not significant enough to indicate a trend.

Obviously, it's difficult to determine a trend when there are so few observations involved, and we might well ask how many additional observations it would take to indicate a probable trend. The total number of observations we need to indicate a trend is given by the formula (Twice sum/Difference)^2, where the sum is the sum of those observations with values above and below the standard mean value, and the difference is the difference between them. In the case of our reject rates on page 70, the sum of our numbers above the mean of 67 (9) and those below (3) is 12 and their difference is 6 (9 − 3). Therefore, $(2 \times 12/6)^2$ equals 16, which is the total number of observations needed in this case to indicate a probable trend. And since we already have 12 observations, this means that we need an additional 4 observations. Of course, the answer may be that there *is* no trend, and you may want to repeat the procedure when you have additional data if you are really looking for one.

TESTING FOR RELATIONSHIPS

Another fundamental concern when dealing with statistical information is detecting cause-and-effect relationships, or correlations, between different factors or variables in the sample and their significance in terms of the population, or reality. These relationships are usually termed "functional" (because one variable is a function of the other), and they can be expressed by a formula or equation. For example, the cost of producing a quantity of a certain product might be said to be a function of the cost per unit times the number of units, or $C = pn$, where C is the total cost, p the cost of producing one unit, and n the total number of units.

This is a *linear* relationship (if you plot the relationship on a graph, it will always come out a straight line). Unfortunately, many of the relationships you will be concerned with cannot be expressed this simply. For example, even in our production example it is obvious there will be certain fixed costs (setup, overhead, etc.) that we shall want to add to the equation. But this can be done without altering the linear nature of the relationship. For example:

$$C = pn + b$$

where b equals the fixed costs.

The difficulty arises when cost per unit goes down as production rises because of greater efficiencies, price breaks in the purchase of raw materials, etc. You then have a *nonlinear* relationship. Such relationships need not be difficult to determine (for example, $C = (pn)^2 + b$ would express such a relationship), but in most cases they are. The point is, the testing of relationships is best left to the expert, who has a number of tools he can use (correlation coefficients, regression analysis, variance analysis, etc.) to get the answer.

FIG. 6.1. Simple Control Chart

SETTING UP THE CONTROLS

The final step in statistical analysis is setting up controls so that you can monitor the events (additional observations) as they occur. And probably the most useful tool in this connection is the graph, or control chart, long used in quality control but useful in many other applications as well, such as sales and production analyses and inventory control. In its simplest form, the control chart might look like that in Figure 6.1.

The advantage of a control chart is that you can immediately see when a situation or operation is getting out of hand and whether there appears to be a trend away from an acceptable norm. In this case we've plotted our 12 observations of the reject rates for department A (see page 70), indicated the acceptable norm of 67 (department B's mean), and arbitrarily set upper and lower limits of 2 standard deviations. Of course, you can set any limits you want, as long as they define your acceptable values, based on sample size. Observations that exceed these limits should be investigated immediately and appropriate action taken to bring the events within the agreed-upon limits. Any time the situation changes, you may want to change the chart, deciding (possibly) upon a new norm and new limits.

7

SHOULD YOU CHANCE IT? . . .

A brief look at probability theory and
the part chance plays in decision-making

As noted a couple of chapters ago, few events are absolutely certain. Their occurrence is only probable. But how probable? *Probability theory* helps us assign numerical values to the likelihood of specific events' occurring. The events with which probability theory concerns itself are characterized as *random,* because their occurrence or outcome is affected by chance. Of course, "chance" is frequently another way of saying that we don't know, or can't calculate, all the causes of an event or its outcome. However, probability theory still applies.

The values assigned to random events are usually expressed in terms of a scale running from 0 (absolute impossibility) through 1.0 (absolute certainty). Thus, if we assign the probability $p = 0.5$ to some event (E), such as heads turning up if we toss a coin, this means that we think the event has a 50 percent chance of actually occurring (on that one toss).

In most cases, the value we assign to an event's probable occurrence is determined statistically, or *empirically*. That is, we assume that an event will continue to occur in the future (given the same conditions) with the same relative frequency with which it has occurred in the past. For example, if we roll a die a large number of times and find that each of the six faces turns up approximately one-sixth of the time, we would be justified in saying that on the next throw the statistical probability of any one of the faces turning up is one-sixth.

Of course, in the case of an unbiased die, it's doubtful if you would go through the long process of determining the probability empirically. Instead, you would probably reason that since there are only six faces and each of them is equally likely to turn up, then the chance of any one turning up *must* be 1 in 6. This is a priori reasoning (reasoning before the fact), and the probability assigned is called an "a priori" probability. But however you determine the probability of an event, you cannot be certain that it will occur with the relative frequency assigned to it. You can only assume that the actual frequency will be close.

SOME BASIC ASSUMPTIONS, OR RULES

In working through more complex problems involving probability, the statistician or mathematician relies on some rather basic assumptions, or rules, governing the relationships between events. These, in turn, are based on the fact that events are either *mutually exclusive* or *independent*. However, some events may be *conditional* upon one another.

For example, a door may be said to be either unlocked (event A) or locked (event B). It cannot be both, so these events are mutually exclusive. If there is a second door whose state of being locked (event B') or unlocked (event A') has nothing whatsoever to do with the state of the first door, then events A' and B' are said to be independent relative to A and B. However, if I wish to open door

2 but must get through door 1 to do so, then the occurrence of event A' will be conditional as far as I am concerned on event A.

The basic rules of probability simply describe the relationships that can exist among these various probabilities. For example, the

sum (S) of all possible mutually exclusive events is unity (certainty). That is to say, $P(S) = 1$. It is assumed, of course, that each of the events has a probability of at least zero $(P[A] \geqq 0)$ and, since the events are mutually exclusive, that $P(AB) = 0$ (i.e., A and B cannot occur at the same time). On this basis, there is a *rule of addition* which states that the probability of any of two or more events occurring is equal to the sum of their individual probabilities. That is to say, if the probability (P) of event A occurring is $P(A)$, and the probability of event B occurring is $P(B)$, then the probability of *either* A *or* B occurring is $P(A) + P(B)$. However, it's important to remember that this rule applies *only* when the events are mutually exclusive.

For example, in the case of the two doors, if there is a 60 percent chance $(p = 0.6)$ of the first door being unlocked and an 80 percent chance $(p = 0.8)$ of the second door being unlocked, the probability of either door 1 or door 2 being unlocked *cannot* be 1.4 (140 percent certain) because, obviously, there is no greater certainty than 1. What complicates the situation in the case of independent events is the fact that there is a possibility that *both* events A and A' can occur simultaneously (it doesn't *have* to be an either/or situation).

When there is the possibility of two events occurring simultaneously, this is expressed symbolically as $P(AB) = P(A) \cdot P(B)$. For example, the probability that *both* doors will be unlocked is $P(A) \cdot P(A')$, or $0.6 \times 0.8 = 0.48$. This is known as the *rule of multiplication*. It applies to successive, as well as simultaneous, occurrences. In point of fact, since I must enter door 1 to get to door 2, the two events are best considered as successive occurrences; and even though they are conditional, the rule still applies.

To express this conditionality symbolically, we would write $P(AA') = P(A) \cdot P(A'/A)$, which is to say that the probability of A and A' both occurring (i.e., finding both doors unlocked) is the probability of A times A', *assuming that* A *in fact occurs*. A and A' are said to be independent when $P(A') = P(A'/A)$. The slant line ($/$) may be roughly translated as "given the occurrence of." This is simply to emphasize the fact that the first event affects the probability of the second event. For example, in the case of the two doors, there is an 80 percent chance of finding the second door unlocked *only* if the first door is unlocked. Otherwise the probability of *finding* the second door unlocked is zero.

Now what we need is a formula that will apply to *general* events A and B (whether mutually exclusive, independent, or conditional). We can get this by combining the rules of addition and multiplication into one general formula: $P(A + B) = P(A) + P(B) - P(AB)$. This is to say, the probability of A or B or both occurring is equal to the probability of A, plus the probability of B, minus the probability of their simultaneous occurrence.

For example, suppose that you manufacture a product from two basic raw materials or ingredients (A and B), obtained from two different sources. There has been a very bad snowstorm which has disrupted delivery of these materials, and your stocks are dangerously low. In fact, if you don't receive shipments of either or both of these materials today, you will have to shut down your plant tomorrow. If there is a 10 percent chance of not getting A and a 20 percent chance of not getting B, what is the probability that you will have to shut down your plant tomorrow? The formula above tells us that the probability that you will have to shut down your plant tomorrow is $0.1 + 0.2 - 0.1 \times 0.2 = 0.28$ (a 28 percent chance of shutdown).

SAMPLE SPACE, SETS, AND VENN

The above rules of probability can be illustrated geometrically by means of what are called "Venn diagrams." While these spatial representations were developed by John Venn for propositional, or symbolic, logic (and we'll meet them again in that connection in a later chapter), they also have mathematical application. This might be the place, therefore, to take a brief look at them, and also at some of the ideas underlying probability.

First of all, we start out with what is called a *sample space* (S), which is symbolized by a rectangle (see Figure 7.1). This is the area within which the possible outcomes we are concerned with can occur. An event in a sample space is considered a *subset*, symbolized by a circle, of that space. An event is said to *occur* when the outcome is a member of that subset.

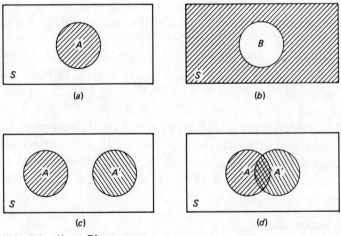

FIG. 7.1. Venn Diagrams

For example, in the Venn diagram (*a*) of Figure 7.1, event A (*door unlocked*) is a member of subset A. All other events (in this case B, *door locked*) lie in the same space outside this area. It is clear from the diagram that an event cannot be a member of subset A and at the same time occur in the non-A (B) area.

Events A and B are therefore mutually exclusive. They are also complementary. This is illustrated by Venn diagram (b). If A has a probability of $p = 0.6$, then B has a probability of $p = 0.4$. The only certain event in this sample space is the occurrence of *either* A *or* B. Or, following the rule of addition, $P(S) = 0.6 + 0.4 = 1$.

Of course, we have been dealing with single events (containing only one member, or element) and with a sample space (a set of possible outcomes) containing only one subset, or event. A sample space may contain many events, and each event may contain many elements. Simple events can be united to obtain all "possible" events in the sample space.

For example, in Venn diagram (c) we have two subsets of single events (A = "finding first door unlocked," A' = "finding second door unlocked"). All other events with which we are concerned (B and B') lie outside these two areas. However, these two single events can be united as in Venn diagram (d) to obtain another "possible" event—finding *both* door 1 and door 2 open.

Following the rule of multiplication, we know that this third event AA' (indicated on the diagram by the cross-hatching) has a probability of $P(AA') = P(A) \cdot P(A')$, where $P(A') = P(A'/A)$. In our example on page 77, $P(AA') = 0.6 \times 0.8 = 0.48$. Venn diagram ($d$) (Figure 7.1) also illustrates the general formula on page 78, where $P(A + B) = P(A) + P(B) - P(AB)$. Or, in this case, $P(A + A') = P(A) + P(A') - P(AA') = 0.6 + 0.8 - 0.48 = 0.92$, which is the probability of one of the three events (A, A', AA') occurring. The complement of this (the event or events lying outside the shaded areas but still within the sample space) is BB', which has a probability of $P(B) \cdot P(B')$, or $0.4 \times 0.2 = 0.08$.

BUILDING REDUNDANCY
INTO A SYSTEM

The basic rules and problems we have so far been considering are all part of what is known as the *mathematical theory of probability*. Essentially they involve counting the number of possible events or outcomes and determining their probabilities, especially as they relate to one another. The more variables (events or outcomes that are possible) involved in a problem, the more complex that problem is generally said to be.

Many of the more complex problems have to do with systems whose functionings depend upon a number of related occurrences. For example, the two doors may be thought of as a system of getting into a plant, and the two ingredients in the snowstorm problem above may be thought of as parts of a system of manufacture. In general, the more complex the system, the greater the likelihood of its being nonoperational (i.e., breaking down).

Since most systems, whether of production or planning or operations (including computers and the human brain), are infinitely more complex than the two-door, two-ingredient systems we mentioned, how then does one keep any such system operational? The answer, of course, is to build redundancy into the system. And the basic laws of probability show why this will reduce failure.

For example, to return to the problem of the two doors as a simple illustration, we found that if you had to return to the plant at night, your chance of getting in (finding both doors unlocked) was 0.48. In essence, this is a two-component system (doors 1 and 2), both components of which must be operating (unlocked) if the system is to function. The system can be diagrammed as in Figure 7.2. There

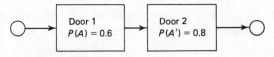

FIG. 7.2. Two-component System

we obtained the probability of the total system being functional by multiplying the probability of door 1 being functional (0.6) by the probability of door 2 being functional (0.8).

Now, your top management, recognizing the fact that it is important for executives to be able to get into the plant at night, is not satisfied with the fact that there is only a 48 percent chance of your getting in when you return to the plant after hours. They therefore install a bell at the outer door which connects with the night watchman's office. If you find door 1 locked, you are instructed to ring the bell and the night watchman will unlock that door for you, although he cannot unlock door 2. However, there is a 0.02 probability that the bell will not work if you ring it, and a 0.7 probability that the watchman will not hear it (since he may be making his rounds). What now is the probability that you will find the system operative (i.e., that you will be able to get in)?

What we have now is a system of components with redundancy built into it. Diagrammed, the system might look like that in Figure 7.3.

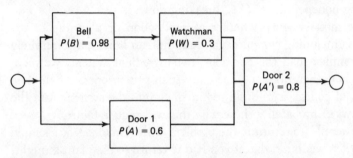

FIG. 7.3.   System with Built-in Redundancy

What now, to repeat, is the probability that the system will be operative if you try to get into the plant at night?

The probability of the lower loop being operative, as indicated, is 0.6. The probability of the upper loop being operative, using the law of multiplication, is $P(BW) = 0.98 \times 0.3 = 0.294$. Both loops do not have to be operative for the total system to be operative, but only either upper or lower, or both. Therefore the general formula applies: The probability of either the upper loop or the lower loop being operative is the sum of the probabilities of both, minus the product of the probabilities of both, or $0.294 + 0.6 - 0.1764 = 0.7176$.

The probability of the total system being operative is now, using the law of multiplication, the probability of either of the loops being operative times the probability of door 2 being operative, or $0.7176 \times 0.8 = 0.57408$. This is a distinct improvement over the previous probability of 0.48. All management has to decide is whether the improvement justifies the cost of the redundancy (in this case, the cost of installing the bell and the inconvenience to the watchman).

COMBINATIONS AND
PERMUTATIONS

Two concepts basic to probability are those of combinations and permutations. When we are concerned with a group of events without any reference to the order in which they occur, we have a problem in *combination*. When we are concerned with the order or arrangement of the events that make up the group, then we have a problem in *permutation*. For example:

If there are nine horses entered in a race, and only the first 3 to come in will pay off, how many different groups of winners can there be? If we manufacture 10 different candies and want to package them in boxes of mixed candies that will hold five different pieces, how many different combinations are possible?

Each of these is a problem in combination, and the answers can be obtained by multiplying the number of objects involved (horses, candies, etc.) by the number of ways the event can occur. In the first problem, for example, there are nine horses, each of which can form part of the winning group in one of three ways (i.e., by placing first, second, or third). Therefore the winning combinations possible are

$$9C3 \, * = \frac{9!}{3!} = \frac{9 \cdot 8 \cdot 7}{3 \cdot 2} = 84$$

In the second problem there are 10 candies that have one in five ways of being chosen to fill the box (i.e., to fill slot 1, 2, 3, 4, or 5). Therefore the answer is

$$\binom{10}{5} = \frac{10!}{5!} = \frac{10 \cdot 9 \cdot 8 \cdot 7 \cdot 6}{5 \cdot 4 \cdot 3 \cdot 2} = 252$$

A permutation, on the other hand, is a combination that has the restriction of order or sequence or arrangement imposed upon it.

* This is the notational shorthand for combinations. In this example it means that the number of ways that combinations of 3 can be taken from 9. For further explanation, see the explanation of permutations on p. 84.

For example, in the horse-racing problem, a winning combination was any group of three horses that placed first, second, or third, regardless of the order. That is, if *A, B,* and *C* are the winning horses, they form only one group, however we arrange them (*ABC, BCA, CBA,* etc.). But if we ask ourselves how many different ways they can be arranged, then we have a problem in permutations.

The answer is obtained by multiplying together the number of ways the event can occur sequentially for each of the objects involved. For example, of the three horses that form a winning combination, one has the possibility of coming in in one of three ways (i.e., first, second, or third); once that occurs, the second horse has the possibility of coming in in one of two ways; and once that occurs, the third horse has only one possibility remaining to it. Therefore, the total number of permutations possible is 3 × 2 × 1 (three choices for the first horse, two for the second horse, one for the third horse) = 6.

If we were concerned with all nine horses in the race and the possibility of each of them forming part of the winning combination of three horses, then the number of permutations would be 9 × 8 × 7 = 504. That is, we have the choice of nine horses to fill the first slot, the choice of eight horses (since one has already been chosen) to fill the second slot, and the choice of seven horses (since two have now been chosen) to fill the third slot in the winning combination.

If we wanted to know the possible permutations of all nine as a group of nine, then the answer is 9 × 8 × 7 × 6 × 5 × 4 × 3 × 2 × 1 = 362,880. In the first case, where we want to know the number of permutations possible for nine things taken three at a time, this is written notationally as 9*P*3. In the second case, where we want to know the number of permutations possible for nine things taken nine at a time, the notation is 9*P*9.*

---

* The formula for determining the total number of permutations is

$$nPr = \frac{n!}{(n-r)!}$$

where *n* is the total number of objects from which *r* number are taken at a time to form a combination. The exclamation mark symbolizes the *factorial*

RANDOM VARIABLES AND
OTHER REFLECTIONS

If the function of statistics is to make statements about the whole based on knowledge of a part, the function of probability is to make statements about a part based on knowledge of the whole.

For example, on the basis of a sample of the population, a statistician might say that 5 percent of the men in America wear bow ties. In terms of probability, however, and based on our knowledge of the entire population, we would say that the chance of the next man we meet wearing a bow tie is 1 in 20. But this distinction sometimes blurs when the problems in probability involve large numbers—where, for instance, we use statistical techniques to determine the probability of a random variable (a variable whose value fluctuates on a random basis) assuming certain values.

For example, if we machine a certain part (say a spindle) on automatic equipment, we would expect to have the part meet specifications within certain tolerances. The variations in actual measurement, if charted, would take on a distribution function, like those discussed in Chapter 5. The probabilities of the parts varying by certain amounts or values from an established norm would be predicated on this distribution, and would be called a *probability density function*. The normal distribution, for instance, would be a probability density function.

Where the probability density function can change with time (e.g., the probability of a piece of equipment failing), a *composite function* (combining several distribution curves) is useful in predicting, say, failure rate. Obviously, also, the function of a random variable, such as the measurements of spindles produced on a cer-

---

of the number it follows. For example, *n factorial* is the product of *n* factors from *n* down to 1, and is written *n*! In the cases above,

$$9P3 = \frac{9!}{(9-3)!} = \frac{9 \cdot 8 \cdot 7 \cdot 6 \cdot 5 \cdot 4 \cdot 3 \cdot 2 \cdot 1}{6 \cdot 5 \cdot 4 \cdot 3 \cdot 2 \cdot 1} = 504, \quad \text{and}$$

$$9P9 = \frac{9!}{(9-9)!} = \frac{9 \cdot 8 \cdot 7 \cdot 6 \cdot 5 \cdot 4 \cdot 3 \cdot 2 \cdot 1}{1} = 362,880$$

Since the definition of *n*! does not apply to $n = 0$, 0! is written as 1.

tain machine, would change as the machine becomes worn. In cases like these, we can determine the composite function from the relative and relative-cumulative frequencies. However, complicated problems like these are best left to the experts. And even the simplest of problems in probability can be mighty tricky.

8

CONCEPTS OF CONTROL . . .

Making sure that things get done

The successful executive is generally thought of as a man who "gets things done." That is, in the popular mind at least, the stress is on the control, or results, end of the management job rather than on deciding what is important and planning how to do it. But what, exactly, is required for effective control? We all know that it takes more than cracking a whip to get things done.

Regardless of the *kind* of situation, or system, we wish to control, whether it be the quality of products on an assembly line, a vast business enterprise or government program, or a household budget, the same four essential elements are involved:

INPUT: Information regarding the objectives we wish the system under control to achieve, how they can be achieved, and standards for measuring the achievement must be fed into the system. OUTPUT: Information about what is actually being accomplished must flow from the system to the control (whether man or machine).

FEEDBACK: The control must measure the output, compare it with the input, and feed this information (if there is a deviation, or error) back into the system.

CORRECTIVE ACTION: Action must be taken to reduce or correct the deviation so as to produce the output desired or (in some cases) to modify the input.

LEVELS OF CONTROL

In the widest sense, what we are talking of is *cybernetics*, the science of man-machine systems of control and communication, first described by Norbert Wiener in "Cybernetics." * Wiener pointed out that the same principles of control that apply in animal life also apply in mechanical systems. In higher animals, for example, the body temperature, blood pressure, and leucocytes must be controlled within strict limits; waste products must be excreted before reaching toxic concentrations; and our sex cycle must conform to society's need for reproduction.

The principle of control used is little different from that of the thermostat, a mechanical device, which is used to regulate the heating system of a house so that the temperature is maintained as desired. However, these control systems work at many different levels within a single organism or organization, though they all utilize the same four essential elements (input, output, feedback, and corrective action). For example, let's look at a ship operating on the high seas.

The helmsman has been given orders to steer the ship on a course of 270 degrees (his input). Waves, wind, and ocean currents, however, throw the ship's heading slightly to the north, so that the actual course is 275 degrees (the output) as measured by the ship's compass. The helmsman notes this deviation of 5 degrees and takes corrective action to bring the ship around to the

* The M.I.T. Press, Cambridge, Mass., 1948.

desired heading (feedback and corrective action). This is simple *tactical* control.

Up in the captain's cabin, the control problem is more of a *managerial* one. The captain is aware that heavy seas are making it unlikely for the ship to reach port at the estimated time of arrival (his input). The navigator arrives to tell the captain that the ship's present position is some 400 miles behind where it should be (output), and recommends changes in course and speed (feedback).

The captain could order these changes to bring output in line with input, but because he considers increased speed too hazardous in heavy seas, he radios a revised arrival estimate to his shipping firm, thus changing his input to conform to results he can realistically hope to achieve.

In the head offices of the shipping firm, the control problem is *strategic*. Let's assume that the ship with our helmsman and captain is a freighter carrying machinery from San Francisco to Honolulu. It is one of a large fleet, and the shipping firm is concerned with ports where there are available cargoes, with destinations for these cargoes, with shipping tariffs, with ships available for charter, with labor expense, with fuel, and with other costs. This is a complex problem, one of selecting and allocating resources in a distribution and transportation situation with more than one kind of inventory (ships, officers, crew, supplies, etc.). But it is also a control problem.

A plan or shipping schedule will be drawn up for optimum utilization of the shipping fleet (to be adjusted from day to day as the variables not under control, such as cargo availability, continue to change). Actual performance of each ship in loading, transporting, and unloading cargoes, in turn-around time, in ship repairs, in loss and damage to cargoes, etc., will be measured and compared with the estimates of time and cost in the shipping schedule. Corrective action to control this kind of strategic situation is more complex than enforcing tactical or managerial controls; it may require admonishing or motivating individual ship captains (each in charge of a profit center) or revising the standards used in developing future schedules, etc.

THE "MULTIPLYING" EFFECT OF CONTROL SYSTEMS

The power of control systems lies in the fact that they enable a small signal to release or contain vast amounts of energy, materials, or information. Thus, a flick of a switch may turn lights on or off, or start up an oil refinery. A few programmed instructions can activate a computer to produce listings of military reserve personnel needed in an emergency. A company president's initials on a memorandum can launch an advertising program for a new product line, stirring the sales force to activity across the country and requiring production from a new plant.

Without the multiplying effect offered by control systems, today's industries and governments could not exist as viable systems. It is only by determining what needs to be accomplished, and establishing controls to achieve those objectives, that large organizations have been able to grow beyond the limits of the individual working on his own or in small units. However, this multiplying effect means that control systems must be designed and built with special care, since an error in the control tends to be multiplied in the system.

The more complex the system to be controlled, the more difficult the control job will be. This is not to say that it is impossible to have effective controls in a large, complex organization—only that it is becoming more and more a job for the systems analyst or operations researcher, who can see the total organization as a single system and judge the ramifications of control systems on all parts of the larger system.

THE FUNCTION OF CONTROLS

However complex the system to which it is applied, the only function of a control is to keep that system operating within certain specified limits. To do this, the control (whether statistical, physiological, mechanical, electrical, budgetary, etc.) tells *when* a decision is necessary (or likely to be necessary) and oftentimes *what* kind of decision is necessary, and in some systems automatically *makes* the decision.

If corrective action is taken automatically (usually when a built-in measuring device detects a deviation from an established range of permissible values for some given activity), such controls are considered *closed*. If, however, the controls merely indicate the need for action by a person or device independent of the system being regulated, they are considered *open*.

Most of the controls with which an executive will be concerned are of the latter variety.

DESIGNING CONTROLS: A
MODEL–BUILDING TASK

When an executive desires to accomplish some end, he usually visualizes the situation and thinks about possible ways to proceed. His image of the situation is, in effect, a model to be manipulated in the planning process. In the same way, designing a control system is a model-building process, and the model must mirror the system it is designed to control.

It should be (1) an accurate and (2) a timely representation of that system. It should be (3) appropriate to the task, and (4) in extent and depth should vary to suit the needs of the system it is to regulate. (You wouldn't, for instance, expect to apply the same controls to the activities of your legal staff as you would to the ful-

fillment of a government contract for a space vehicle component.)
The control system should be (5) worth the cost and, finally, (6)
the factors selected for control should be ones that are critical to the
system.

Special attention is required with the use of averages in constructing standards and indices for control purposes. In many cases
optimum performance data may be more reliable than averages.
According to Stafford Beer,* optimums reflect fundamental relationships more accurately than do averages. The overriding merit
of a model constructed from optimum data is that it is more likely
to be valid for the future.

Similar care needs to be taken with the use of performance indices. The project that is halfway (50 percent) through its performance schedule and has expended half (50 percent) its budgeted
funds might be right on target in its progress/expenditure ratio
(100 percent). Yet this index may conceal the fact that the project
is only half completed (a critical failure)—so that reporting that
expenditures are in line with progress is relatively unimportant and
even deceptive.

Of course, few systems have one neat control designed to make
the system perform perfectly. In fact, in any organizational system
there will probably be as many controls as there are objectives. For
example, sales quotas reflect marketing objectives; production schedules reflect manufacturing goals. You are no doubt familiar with
traditional controls, such as budgets, progress reports, quality controls, return on investment, and cost accounting. In addition, in re-
cent years highly effective techniques have been developed for
project control that are commanding widespread attention in industry and government.

MAJOR CONTROL TECHNIQUES:
THE CRITICAL PATH METHOD

Until the late 1950s, the most commonly accepted means of planning and controlling projects was the Gantt chart, essentially a bar

* "Decision and Control," John Wiley & Sons, Inc., New York, 1966.

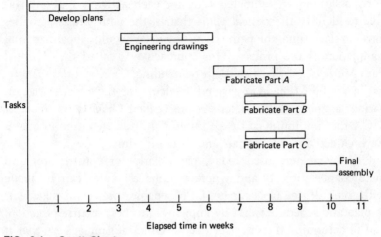

FIG. 8.1.   Gantt Chart

chart indicating progress of the work, by task, expressed in units of time. Figure 8.1, for example, is a typical Gantt chart.

E. I. DuPont de Nemours & Co. improved the Gantt technique by adding a description of relationships among the various activities. The sequence of activities was shown in an *arrow network*, so called because it gave the direction of these relationships. For any given relationship (call it operation X), these three questions would be answered: Which operation must immediately precede operation X? Which operations can be performed at the same time as X? Which operation cannot start until X is completed? The arrow network, considerably simplified, looked something like Figure 8.2.

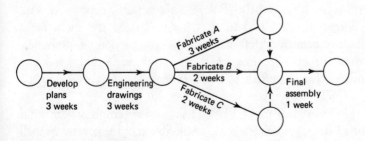

FIG. 8.2.   Arrow Network

By assigning an estimated time for each activity, DuPont was able to identify the *critical path*—that is, the path whose activities have no slack time, the path where any delay would jeopardize final completion of the project. This approach was called the "Critical Path Method" (or "Critical Path Scheduling," "Critical Path Analysis," etc.). CPM made provision for calculating the effect of cost on various activities, and a later version (called CPM-II by some, or MCX for "minimum-cost expediting") utilized *two* time estimates for each activity—a "normal" and a "crash" time.

CPM is widely used today, particularly for construction and maintenance projects and wherever time estimates can be made with some degree of accuracy. CPM enables project management to plan and schedule work, by knowing the "best" course of action, and to determine the effect of delays. Other advantages are that it gives all personnel involved in the project a clear picture of what is going on, it makes management-by-exception possible, it makes possible the control of projects hitherto considered too unwieldy, and it makes quick rescheduling of a project possible if changing conditions require it.

MAJOR CONTROL TECHNIQUES: PROGRAM EVALUATION AND REVIEW TECHNIQUE

Shortly after CPM appeared, the Navy developed PERT (Program Evaluation and Review Technique) with the help of the management consulting firm of Booz, Allen & Hamilton, in order to coordinate and control some 250 prime contractors and over 9,000 subcontractors in the Polaris submarine weapons system. PERT differed from CPM in that it emphasized the moment at which events occurred that marked the completion of activities, rather than the elapsed time for those activities. Nor did it make any provision for the effect of costs, though a later version, called PERT/COST, does take costs into account.

The significant feature of PERT has been its emphasis on rapid detection of delay, which makes it a valuable tool for control as well as planning. This is attributable to PERT's weighted time esti-

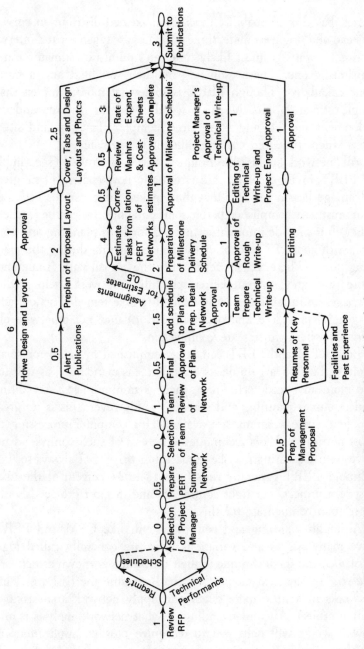

FIG. 8.3. Sample PERT Network (Research Institute of America)

mates, based on probability theory and skewed distribution curves. Instead of a single estimate, *three* estimates are given for the interval between events: a most likely time, an optimistic estimate, and a pessimistic one. These estimates are then weighted and a mean time calculated. Though PERT is somewhat more complex than single-estimate approaches, it is widely used for research and development projects and other large, complex, first-of-a-kind situations where time and cost are difficult to estimate.

All "network analysis" techniques, as they are called (see sample of PERT in Figure 8.3), are essentially flow charts. Their great advantage lies in the fact that they make visible various activities that must be accomplished before some end objective can be reached. They thus provide information needed for both planning and control, with about 75 percent of the benefit coming during the planning phase. These techniques identify the critical path (sometimes more than one), permit better scheduling of work, help predict slippages and their effect early enough to take remedial action, and in general provide a knowledge of performance not otherwise obtainable when projects are complicated.

Both CPM and PERT can be accomplished by hand for small projects, but for large projects a computer is mandatory, as it is for the more advanced techniques, such as minimum-cost expediting and resources planning and scheduling. However, this is no great problem, since programs are available for computer processing of most network analysis techniques. The cost of such controls as we have been discussing may be modest, but this is not always so. For example, PERT generally runs from $1\frac{1}{2}$ to $3\frac{1}{2}$ percent of the total cost of a project. Yet tight control of time in most projects should more than compensate for this.

Although planning and control systems like CPM and PERT have many names and variations, they are generally called *logic networks,* and the technique of their utilization is known as *network analysis.* In the next chapter we shall examine the basics of logic networks in a little more detail and apply network analysis to a simple project. An understanding of what network analysis is and how it works will help you to recognize possible applications to problems within your own organization.

9

BRANCHES IN A PATTERN . . .

How logic networks and network analysis help systematize planning and control

Essentially, logic networks such as PERT or CPM are simply a means of getting the activities involved in a project in the right order by the use of an analog or a diagrammatic plan. These plans, or networks, are composed of three basic symbols: *arrows* to represent activities, *nodes* or small circles to represent events, and *dashed-line arrows* to represent dummy, or zero, activities (activities that take up no time or resources).

In creating logic networks, no attempt is made to draw them to scale. The time flow is generally from left to right, as indicated by the arrows. The actual passage of time (usually expressed in weeks) is indicated by the numbers above the arrows.

Each activity begins and ends in an event, symbolized by the small circle. These circles usually have reference numbers in them.

Events simply mark points in time when activities can begin or end, and take no time themselves. Nor do the dummy, or zero, activities take any time; the dashed-line arrows are drawn in simply to show that certain activities are dependent upon them (i.e., the dummy activities must be completed before others can be begun).

A logic network, then, is just what the name implies: a diagram in the form of a network that shows the logical relationships between the various activities involved in completing a project. One activity cannot be begun until the event preceding it has occurred, and an event cannot occur until all activities (including zero activities) leading to it are complete. Although networks can involve the use of subtle mathematical techniques, particularly in the estimation of time, the essential discipline required is logical analysis.

PLANNING A PERT NETWORK: WORK BREAKDOWN SCHEDULE

As with anything else that an executive undertakes, the first step in planning a PERT network is to ask what he hopes to achieve (i.e., What are the major and minor objectives?). To help in de-

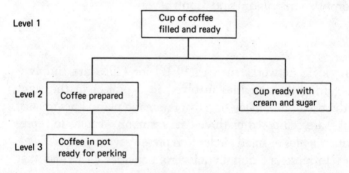

FIG. 9.1. PERT Work Breakdown Schedule

termining this, some planners use what is called a *work breakdown schedule,* starting with the major objective and working backward through time, listing each of the subobjectives in a top-to-bottom order. Figure 9.1, for example, shows how such a schedule might look if our major objective were to prepare and drink a cup of coffee.

The next step in planning a PERT network is to list all the activities we can think of that might be involved in achieving these objectives, starting at the bottom with the subobjectives. For example:

Get electric coffee pot and fill with water.
Get coffee and put in pot.
Plug in coffee pot and allow to perk.

Get cup, saucer, and spoon.
Get sugar and put in cup.
Get cream and put in cup.
Pour coffee in cup and stir.
Drink coffee.

CREATING A PERT NETWORK

Once we've listed all the activities we can think of, and arranged them in some kind of logical sequence, we're ready to begin actually drawing our first crude network (refining it as we go along to include activities we might have overlooked, etc.). But the first thing that will strike you in trying to diagram the situation (and this is typical of PERT projects) is that, although the situation is essentially serial, many things occur in parallel.

In the coffee project, for example, it is obvious that some of the activities in the right-hand column are going to be carried on simultaneously with some of the activities in the left-hand column. In effect, we have two main streams of activities, occupying the same time continuum, that will have to merge before the final objective is achieved, and each can be represented by a subnetwork. (For example, see Figure 9.2.)

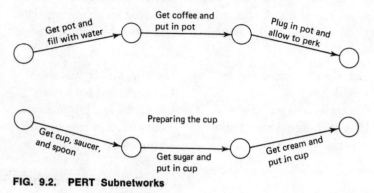

FIG. 9.2. PERT Subnetworks

All we have to do, after creating each of the subnetworks, is to join them at the points where they have events in common (these are called *interface events*) and complete the network. This is essentially what is done when you buy "packaged" networks that have been previously programmed for computers. For example, if we put our two subnetworks together, we get a master network that might look something like that shown in Figure 9.3.

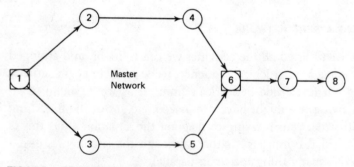

FIG. 9.3. PERT Master Network

The diagram in Figure 9.3 is the master network for our coffee project—but instead of labeling each activity, we have numbered the events in the accepted west-to-east, north-to-south directions. By assigning a number to each activity based on the events that begin and end it (e.g., the activity of getting the pot and filling it with

Activity no.	Activity description	Event no. and description	
1-2	Get pot and fill with water	1	Initiate project
1-3	Get cup, saucer, and spoon	2	Pot filled with water
2-4	Get coffee and put in pot	3	Cup, saucer, and spoon ready
3-5	Get sugar and put in cup	4	Coffee in pot
4-6	Allow coffee to perk	5	Sugar in cup
5-6	Get cream and put in cup	6	Coffee perked and cream in cup
6-7	Pour coffee in cup and stir	7	Coffee in cup and stirred
7-8	Drink coffee	8	Coffee drunk

FIG. 9.4. PERT Activities and Events

water is now 1-2), we can prepare a description of the activities and events as in Figure 9.4.

REFINING OUR NETWORK: LOGICAL RELATIONSHIPS AND RESOURCES

So far we have given no thought to either time or resources in preparing our network. This is an important procedure to follow. In the beginning you are to consider logical relationships only, *and timing afterward;* then, if the timing is not acceptable or the resources are not available, you can begin, in a *systematic* way, to alter the network. For example, in the network shown in Figure 9.3 there are a couple of logical inconsistencies.

First, because of our limited resources (namely, the fact that there may be one worker only), it is not likely that we can begin *both* activities 1-2 and 2-3 at the same time. It would seem, then, that we have two choices open to us: we can either get another worker to carry on one activity while we carry on the other, or we can schedule one activity to follow the other. Which choice we should make and, if the latter, which activity should follow which, are decisions that might best be founded upon time considerations—and possibly costs, if we are utilizing CPM.

In the second place, event 6 is *not* a true interface event. It is not necessary, nor is it important, that activities 4-6 and 5-6 end at the same point in time.* Therefore, let us try a new network.

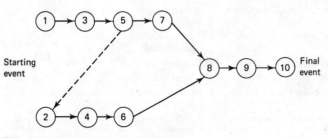

FIG. 9.5. Revised Master Network

The revised master network in Figure 9.5 makes clearer the logical relationships between activities and the dependencies of the various events. In the first place, the true interface event (8) is now indicated instead of the false one we had before. And in the second

* This, in general, is how one goes about refining a network: by questioning every step, every decision, and making sure that every dependency is real. Hence the name, network *analysis*.

Activity no.	Activity description	Event no. and description	
1-3	Get pot and fill with water	3	Pot filled with water
2-4	Get cup, saucer, and spoon	4	Cup, saucer and spoon ready
3-5	Get coffee and put in pot	5	Coffee in pot
4-6	Get sugar and put in cup	6	Sugar in cup
5-2	Dummy activity showing that event 2 is not to start until event 5 has occurred		
5-7	Allow coffee to perk	7	Coffee perked
6-8	Get cream and put in cup	8	Cream and coffee in cup
7-8	Pour coffee in cup		
8-9	Stir coffee	9	Coffee stirred
9-10	Drink coffee	10	Coffee finished

FIG. 9.6. Revised Activities and Events

place, we have added a dummy, or zero, activity to indicate a dependency that might have been overlooked before. But now, of course, we need a new table of activities and events (Figure 9.6).

REFINING OUR NETWORK: TIME CONSIDERATIONS

The network now looks logically consistent and within the limitations of our resources—but we can't really be sure until we take the important step of estimating the time for each activity and, consequently, the overall time for our project. In a PERT network, time is our basic measure of the work required to complete the project. It is usually expressed in calendar weeks, but in our example we shall use minutes. Time in calendar weeks, of course, is determined by dividing the number of working days per week into the number of working days required.

In diagramming a PERT, CPM network, we are concerned with *two* sets of time: the earliest event time (EET) and the latest event time (LET). Our nodes are now redrawn to look like those in Figure 9.7.

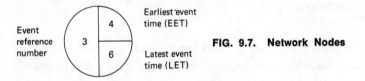

Event reference number

4 Earliest event time (EET)

3

6 Latest event time (LET)

FIG. 9.7.   Network Nodes

To figure earliest event times, we start with zero time for the first event and add the activity time (based, as indicated on page 96, on *three* estimates incorporated into a weighted formula) to each preceding event time, until we arrive at the final event. This figure will then be the total estimated time for the project. Of course, where two activity paths lead into one event, the path with the *longest* activity time should be selected in determining event time.

To figure the latest event times, we assume that the latest event time and the earliest event time at the final event are the same. We then work *back* through the network, subtracting the activity times from the latest event time at each node to determine the latest event time at the preceding node. But this time, when the tails of two or more activity paths originate at an event, the path with the *lowest* time (dummy activities excepted) is selected to determine the latest event time at that node. To illustrate, Figure 9.8 shows our network with both the EET and LET indicated at each node. If you will work forward from the starting event to determine EET and back from the final event to determine LET, you will see how it works.

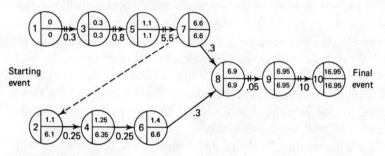

FIG. 9.8. Network with Times Indicated

ANALYZING OUR NETWORK: EVENT SLACK AND ACTIVITY FLOAT

Where there is a difference between the earliest and latest event times at a node, this is known as "event slack." This is the period of time during which the event *must* occur if the final event (i.e., the project) is to occur at the time indicated. For example, at event 6 in Figure 9.8 above, the slack time is equivalent to 5.2 minutes, which means that event 6 can happen anywhere from 1.4 to 6.6 minutes after the starting event. Obviously, there is a lot of slack built into the system at this point, and the activity immediately preceding it is not likely to cause trouble.

Another important concept in analyzing a network, similar to event slack, is called *activity float*. This is the difference between the earliest event time at the beginning of an activity and the latest event time at the conclusion of the activity minus the duration time of the activity, as shown on your network. For example, activity 4-6 has float of 4.95 minutes (the difference between an EET of 1.4 and a LET of 6.6, minus activity time of 0.25). In essence, this means that activity 4-6 can be delayed or stretched out by 4.95 minutes without delaying the project as a whole. In general, the larger the float, the less important that activity is to the total project as far as time is concerned.

ANALYZING OUR NETWORK:
THE CRITICAL PATH

The longest path through the network (there may be more than one) is known as the *critical path*. It is that path which, from starting event to final event, is the most time-consuming. It can be identified by the fact that none of the events along that path have slack time, and none of the activities have float. In Figure 9.8 above we have identified the critical path by drawing a pair of hash marks on each of the activity vectors along the path that is critical. This path is critical, because a delay in any of the activities or events along it will result in a proportionate delay in the project.

At this point, of course, our network analysis is far from complete. In fact, logic networks must be thought of as dynamic processes rather than as static tools. They are useful in control as well as planning, and any time during the course of a project that activity times differ from estimated times we would want to check the network for possible refinement or correction. Since, in a PERT network, our major consideration is time, the basic question is: Are we utilizing our time as effectively as we might? The basic assumption is that effective use of our time will tend to maximize resources and minimize costs.

ANALYZING OUR NETWORK:
REPLANNING AND ADJUSTMENT

Looking at the network in Figure 9.8, we might well wonder whether the total project time of 16.95 minutes is satisfactory. Suppose, for instance, that our coffee break is limited to a maximum of 15 minutes, giving us an overrun of almost 2 minutes. Is there anything we can do to shorten it? Obviously, there isn't—unless we deduct time from one or more of the activities along the critical path, for savings in time elsewhere are not likely to affect total time. To determine if adjustment is possible, here are three questions to ask:

1. *Can we relax some of the limitations, specifications, or restrictions?* For example, the two major time consumers are activities 5-7 (coffee perking) and 9-10 (drinking coffee). Could we settle for coffee that is not fully perked by lowering our standards for drinkable coffee? If *yes,* we can save some time on activity 5-7. Must you take a full 10 minutes to drink your coffee? By gulping it a little while it is still hot, you may be able to save time on activity 9-10. In the same way, examine the other activities.

2. *Can we shift some of our resources (men, money, machines, material, etc.) around to effect savings in time?* For example, by using a cheaper coffee, we might be able to invest the savings in a faster coffee-maker, reducing time on activity 5-7. Or if this were a more typical project involving more workers, maybe we could shift them from activities with float to critical-path activities, if there is sufficient float to permit this. This would *increase* the duration of the noncritical activities but *decrease* the duration of the critical activities—thus reducing total project time.

3. *Can we rearrange the activities in the network?* In our coffee project example, if we did buy a new coffee-maker to save a little time (let's say it was a Silex vacuum type), we perhaps could make further reductions in time by rearranging activities. For example, we could shift activity 5-7 ahead of 3-5, and complete 3-5 while 5-7 was occurring. In other words, we could put the coffee in the pot while the water was coming to a boil, and save the time of that activity (0.8 minutes). In effect, we would move activity 3-5 to the noncritical path, preceding event 2.

LIMITATIONS OF PERT, CPM, AND OTHER NETWORKS

CPM adds time-cost relationships to those we have been considering; otherwise it is very similar to PERT. But *all* versions of

CPM and PERT have one flaw: they do not take into account the fact that resources may be limited (they assume that all the necessary manpower and materials are on hand). However, a host of related techniques have been developed since for specialized situations, and some of these (for example, RAMPS—developed by Coir, Inc. and ASTRA—developed by General Electric) consider the effect of resources available within the organization upon time, cost, and the critical path.

But whichever network or other system you choose for planning and control, the essentials are that it should be representative of the system it regulates and that it should measure those factors that are critical to the system. In addition, it should require reports or other feedback, corrective action should be taken to the extent called for in the system, and the networks or other controls should be modified just as soon as the system it governs starts to change.

10

QUICKEN THE QUEUE . . .

How to handle the waiting customer faster and better

Waiting lines, as you are well aware, are everywhere: in retail stores, manufacturing plants, bowling alleys, government agencies, schools, restaurants, you name it. And every executive, no matter how prestigious, has at one time or another waited in *some* line, for *some* service. So you're undoubtedly familiar with the problem and realize its essential simplicity: Customers arrive, and demand service. Depending upon the service available, either the customers wait or the facilities are idle. The trick is to balance demand against service, thus minimizing total cost (the cost of having a line versus the cost of idle time).

Waiting lines needn't be told to form: they often form themselves. Basically, they are an organizational device, a discipline invented by either the organization or the customers to define the order of service. If Adams is alone at the bus stop, he's first in line (he claims). Baker walks up, becoming number two. Most such queues organized by customers have a first-come, first-served discipline. But if Caroline shows up just as the bus comes along, gentlemen Adams and Baker may recognize her priority (in some localities they may not). In any event, typical waiting lines include not just people but trucks waiting to be loaded, papers in an "In" basket waiting to be processed, items on magnetic tape waiting to be read by a computer, semifinished items awaiting a final finishing step, etc.

In short, you have a waiting-line problem if something or someone (a customer, a work unit, a batch of papers, or materials in process) arrives and demands service, and if, because of irregular arrival times, batching or idleness occurs. In most waiting-line situations, the arrivals are *not* subject to control, but the service facilities *are*. This has the pattern of a typical OR problem. If you will recall, we said that the effectiveness of any system is a function of the variables subject to control and the variables not subject to control. In most waiting-line situations, the variables subject to our control are the service facilities.

WHY A WAITING LINE?

Waiting lines can exist for a variety of reasons. The military, for example, has been known to use waiting lines to teach recruits patience. Young doctors are not above bunching their patients into a few hours in the morning to give the impression of busy success.

Even in a plant or office, a moderate backlog of work can be a good thing—psychologically. Time studies have shown, according to the Research Institute of America, that workers on an assembly line will tend to increase their output when they actually see work waiting for them. In short, waiting lines can have important psychological effects.

But although waiting lines may serve other purposes, they exist (and their existence is justified) in most normal situations for one very important reason: it is usually cheaper to have a line than *not* to have a line. And the length of the line (or the amount of time each unit may have to wait to be serviced) that is most economical can be determined by OR and regulated by the facilities provided to service the line. Let's look at a typical queuing situation, describing it in OR terminology.

JOE THE BARBER: ORGANIZED FOR SERVICE

When Joe first opened for business, he put in three barber chairs (anticipating future growth), although *he* provided the only serv-

ice. (On a busy day he might have a customer in the chair and three others waiting.) His shop was an example of the most elementary queue: a single waiting line with a first-come, first-served discipline and a *single-channel, single-phase* operation. Diagrammed, it looked like Figure 10.1.

Waiting line   Channel   Service

O   O   O   O ————————————▶ D (Joe)

FIG. 10.1.   Diagram of Single-channel, Single-phase Operation

As business grew, Joe hired another barber (Tony), and the shop now offered a *multichannel* service (Figure 10.2).

Finally, business was so good that Joe was able to hire a second barber (Nick) to take over the third chair. At the same time, it occurred to Joe that maybe he could run a more efficient operation if

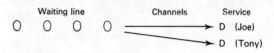

FIG. 10.2. Multichannel Service

each of the barbers specialized (he would give the shaves, Tony the haircuts, and Nick the shampoos). Organized this way, his shop became a *three-phase, sequential* operation (because the customers were serviced in sequence), with a single channel and waiting still on a first-come, first-served basis (Figure 10.3).

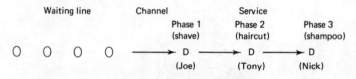

FIG. 10.3. Three-phase, Sequential Operation

However, it quickly became obvious that this wouldn't work—for the simple reason that not all customers wanted or needed all three services, and thus units (customers) were kept waiting needlessly at service facilities they didn't intend to utilize. And even if all the arrivals required all three phases of the service, the average service time for each phase was different, with the result that one barber might be very busy while another was idle, and the waiting lines would then be inefficient (i.e., either too long or too short). Allowing the customers to determine their own sequence (order of service) alleviated the problem somewhat, but obviously failed to provide an optimum solution because of inequality in the demand for each phase of the service.

Joe therefore went back to a single-phase operation, with each barber offering each customer from a single line any or all services. This solution seemed to satisfy Joe, but whether it is optimum or not we don't know. We've made no attempt at an OR solution, and we doubt if Joe has even considered all the strategies available to him that might provide a "good enough" solution to his (or to any) waiting-line problem. Let's look at some of these before considering a queuing problem that is more useful for our purposes in illustrating the application of OR.

PRELIMINARY WAITING–LINE STRATEGICS: THE SERVICE FACILITIES

Since, in any waiting-line situation, the variable most subject to our control is the service we provide, this is obviously the first (and frequently the only) place to look for a solution. Here are some questions you might ask before you decide to call in an analyst:

■ *Can you reduce the service time?* When a waiting line gets long, a slight cut in average service time can bring dramatic improvement, particularly when arrivals are random. But speeding up service, if it means a decline in quality or a pace that cannot be maintained, can only be a temporary solution (but it may be that the *problem* is only temporary).

■ *Can you reduce the variation in service time?* On the other hand, when arrivals have an even rate (as on an assembly line), variations in service will frequently prove to be inefficient. For example, if units arrive for service every five minutes and it takes $4\frac{1}{2}$ minutes to service each unit on the average, wide variations in service time required by each of your customers can get you hopelessly behind.

■ *Can you increase the number of service channels?* If the line at one service facility gets too long, can you switch the customers to another facility via a second channel? The efficiency of Joe the barber's final solution, for example, lay mostly in the fact that it provided for three channels from a single line.

■ *Can you reduce the number of phases?* Occasionally a multiphase operation will be more efficient than a single-phase one (and often it's not possible to avoid it), but as a general rule the fewer the phases, the more efficient the service will be—witness Joe's attempt at a multiphase operation.

PRELIMINARY WAITING–LINE STRATEGIES: THE CUSTOMERS

The second place to look for a solution is in the arrivals. We have said that this is the variable *not* subject to our control—but that is not always strictly so. In an assembly-line situation, for example, the arrivals can frequently be controlled to *some* extent, and any queuing problems that arise may therefore be solved more quickly and easily (although there are apt to be other problems). Strictly speaking, we really have a queuing problem only to the extent that the arrivals *are* random and uncontrollable. Here, then, are questions you might ask concerning the customer when faced with a waiting-line situation:

■ *Can you reduce the arrival rate?* Can you persuade the customer to accept a different service, perhaps even discourage his arrival? A theater does this, for instance, when it puts out an SRO sign.

■ *Can you vary the arrival times?* Can you stagger the incoming units, or shift customers to an off-peak period? A store, for example, can do this by having sale days; a barber shop does this by charging more for a haircut on Saturdays.

■ *Can you vary the batch size?* If arrivals come in batches, can you break them up (send incoming mail to the various departments, for example, before opening it), or discourage large batching (a restaurant can do this, for example, by insisting upon reservations for groups above a certain size)?

■ *Can you predict and therefore prepare for the arrival rate?* In many businesses it's possible to predict peak demand. The maternity ward in a hospital, for example, gets an advance indication of the need for its services through the obstetricians who are connected with it.

A TYPICAL WAITING–LINE PROBLEM

In short, there are many strategies you can try before deciding that you have a waiting-line problem that calls for the application of

OR techniques. Typically, the problem requiring OR will involve a single waiting line on a first-come, first-served basis, the customers will arrive at random, the service time will vary, and the service rate will be greater than the arrival rate (if it weren't, the need for additional facilities would be too obvious to require OR—except, perhaps, to determine how many or how much).

In many cases, the arrival rate will slow as the waiting line increases. For example, every customer who comes to the door of Joe's barber shop will enter for service if there is no one waiting; but if one person is waiting, maybe only 9 out of 10 will enter; if 2 persons are waiting, maybe only 7 out of 10 will enter, etc.; until eventually a point is reached where the waiting line is so long that no new arrivals will enter the shop for service.

In many instances, also, the service rate will increase with an increase in the line (i.e., less time will be spent servicing each unit so that more units can be serviced). For example, if Joe has no waiting line in his shop, he may spend 20 minutes giving a customer a haircut; but if there is a line, he may be able to decrease the service time as the line increases, to the point where he may be spending 10 minutes per haircut, and servicing customers at the rate of 6 per hour instead of 3.

ARRIVAL RATES AND SERVICE RATES

The ratio between the arrival rate and the service rate is an essential consideration in solving queuing problems, and their variability can complicate what might otherwise be a rather more simple problem. But as a general rule, when the ratio of arrival rate to service rate (often called the *traffic intensity*, or *load factor*) is very low, so is the waiting line; and, in most cases, when the ratio reaches about 0.7 to 0.8, the waiting line begins to rise sharply, approaching infinity (theoretically, at least) as the ratio approaches 1.

Here are the formulas that tell us the average length of the waiting line and the average time each customer must wait to be serviced—if we know the average arrival rate and the service rate for the operation under study. (However, they apply only to a single service facility; there are other formulas for parallel service facilities, or for service facilities in series.)

Average waiting-line length =
$$\frac{(\text{average arrival rate})^2}{\text{service rate} \times (\text{service rate} - \text{arrival rate})}$$

Average waiting time =
$$\frac{\text{average arrival rate}}{\text{service rate} \times (\text{service rate} - \text{arrival rate})}$$

The first formula says that you can find what the average length of your waiting line will be if you square the average arrival rate and divide this by the service rate times the arrival rate minus the service rate. For example, if on the average 8 customers or units arrive each hour to be serviced, and we can service 10 per hour, then the average length of our waiting line will be 3.2 customers.

$$\text{Average waiting-line length} = \frac{8^2}{10(10 - 8)} = \frac{64}{20} = 3.2$$

Obviously, this occurs only to the extent that the arrivals are completely random—and it is also obvious that the service facilities are going to be idle for some part of that hour. When the arrivals are random, some of them will occur in batches, thus accounting for the waiting. If an arrival occurred every 6 to $7\frac{1}{2}$ minutes, there would be no waiting (since servicing takes only 6 minutes), and the service facilities would be idle for 12 minutes out of every hour.

The average time that each customer or unit has to wait to be serviced can be found by dividing the average arrival rate by the average service rate times service rate minus arrival rate. In the example above, the average is 0.4 (8 divided by 20) of an hour, or 24 minutes. Is this good or bad? Is it costing us customers? Maybe we should add another service facility. But we are already paying for 12 minutes of idle time each hour! In short, this kind of analysis is only the beginning, and the figures are meaningless unless they relate to an actual situation. So let's look at one.

THE CASE OF ELLA, THE
TELEPHONE GIRL

At the Little Wonder Manufacturing Company, orders are frequently telephoned in to a special order clerk named Ella. Although Ella was a whiz when she was first hired (she could take a telephone order in six minutes on the average), she's in trouble now. Recently, customers have complained that they can't get orders through, and the switchboard operator claims that Ella's line is always busy. Ella's boss, Sam Smith, thinks she should be able to handle ten incoming calls an hour (since each one averages only six minutes) and suspects that she's wasting too much time in idle chatter with the other girls.

Sam happens to mention the problem to Oliver Randall, a young OR analyst who has recently joined the company, and Ollie immediately comes to Ella's rescue. He points out that if she *did* get 10 calls an hour, the waiting line would stretch to infinity (at least in theory). As it is, with eight incoming calls an hour (according to records kept by the switchboard operator), Ollie figures (using the formulas on page 116) that better than three calls (3.2, to be exact) will be waiting for Ella at any one time, and that the average customer will have to wait 24 minutes before getting through to Ella. Add the six minutes of service time to that, and it takes the average customer a half-hour to place a telephone order with Little Wonder.

"Ridiculous!" Sam snorts. "No customer will spend half an hour to place an order with us. And I don't think there's any such thing as an *infinite* waiting line."

"You're right," Ollie agrees. "The queue never really gets very big, because many of your customers undoubtedly just give up and either try again or order from the competition. In other words, the line is self-limiting."

"Let's get the facts," Sam says, and Ollie starts keeping track of the number of incoming calls, how long each waits, and how long it takes for service. He develops a frequency distribution showing the pattern of incoming call rates and another pattern of service

Average number of incoming calls per hr	Average potential service rate per hr	Traffic intensity	Expected number of calls waiting to be connected	Expected waiting time of average customer before being connected, min
2	10	0.2	0.05	1.5
3	10	0.3	0.13	2.6
4	10	0.4	0.27	4.1
5	10	0.5	0.50	6.0
6	10	0.6	0.90	9.0
7	10	0.7	1.63	14.0
8	10	0.8	3.20	24.0
9	10	0.9	8.10	54.0
10	10	1.0	∞	∞

FIG. 10.4.   Incoming Calls, Potential Service, Traffic Intensity, etc.

time variations. He then figures what the waiting-line length and average waiting time would be for varying incoming phone call rates, and prepares a chart like that in Figure 10.4.

Of course, this is purely theoretical, since, as Ollie found out through monitoring the incoming calls, some customers refused to wait at all, few were willing to wait beyond six minutes, and none were willing to wait more than 10 minutes. The practical result of this self-limiting factor was that, while the switchboard operator received eight calls on an average for Ella each hour, only five of the customers actually reached Ella for servicing. And since (to keep the problem simple) none of these customers ever called back, the company was losing three orders per hour, each of which would have meant an average profit of $10. This queuing problem, therefore, was costing the company $30 an hour, or $1,200 a week.

THE CASE OF ELLA: SHOULD THEY HIRE ANOTHER GIRL?

Since the cost of adding another special order clerk would be only $120 a week (this includes salary, fringe benefits, office space, etc.), the logic of the situation seemed to dictate doing so. But Ollie wasn't about to advise that yet—not, that is, until they had considered some of the other strategies available to them, strategies like those listed on pages 113–114. So, as a good analyst should, Ollie sat down with Sam and together they went over the service facility to see what they could do about improving it. They came up with the following idea.

Instead of writing up the customer's name and address for each order, couldn't Ella keep a file of pre-stenciled order forms? And couldn't Ella use the production department's code numbers for the make and model of each product ordered (they put the code numbers on in production, anyway—the next step in the process)? They tried the idea and found that the new form enabled Ella to take a telephone order in *three* minutes on the average, a theoretical service rate of 20 orders an hour. By doubling the rate, Sam figured, the waiting time should be cut in half. But he is in for a surprise.

When service time is cut in half (from 6 minutes to 3), waiting time is cut even more. For 8 incoming calls an hour, waiting time drops from 24 minutes to only 2, one-twelfth of what it was before. Sam is delighted, thinks Ollie is a genius, and everybody is happy, including Ella. But business picks up, and inside of a year better

Average number of incoming calls per hr	Average potential service rate per hr	Traffic intensity	Expected number of calls waiting to be connected	Expected waiting time of average customer before being connected, min
2	20	0.10	0.01	0.33
4	20	0.20	0.05	.0.75
6	20	0.30	0.13	1.29
8	20	0.40	0.27	2.00
10	20	0.50	0.50	3.00
12	20	0.60	0.90	4.50
14	20	0.70	1.63	7.00
15	20	0.75	2.25	9.00
16	20	0.80	3.20	12.00
18	20	0.90	8.10	27.00
20	20	1.00	∞	∞

FIG. 10.5. **Revised Traffic Intensity and Service Chart**

than 15 calls an hour are coming through the switchboard for Ella, and the waiting line (waiting time, too) has grown to the point where it is costing them a considerable amount of business. Ollie takes another look at the situation (Figure 10.5).

THE CASE OF ELLA: WHAT ABOUT THE ARRIVALS?

There didn't seem to be anything more they could do about the service, so this time Ollie and Sam tackle the arrival problem. "Why can't some of the customers fill in the order form themselves?" they ask. "If we printed up some order forms for each customer on postcards, with the customer's name and address preprinted, and if the cards were preaddressed straight to our plant, wouldn't it encourage some of the customers to order by mail rather than by telephone? We could even offer the customer a 1 percent discount on postcard orders and still come out ahead."

It seemed worth a try, and (surprise!) the new approach eliminates about one-half the incoming calls, which are more than compensated for by postcard orders. Again, everything is fine . . . for about six months. But gradually business doubles. Postcard orders are still coming in at the same rate, but telephone calls for Ella have climbed back up to an arrival rate of about 15 per hour. What to do? It appears that the time has come to hire that extra girl. But no . . .

Ollie notices that telephone congestion occurs during only three hours of the day, in the morning from 11:00 to 12:00 and in the afternoon from 3:00 to 5:00. Out goes a notice to customers that incoming phone orders will be subject to a 1 percent discount if made before 10:30 A.M. or between 1:00 and 2:30 P.M. This smoothing out of the arrival rate cuts the waiting time again, and things are fine for another few months. But with the next spurt in business, Ollie finally gives up.

"We can't put off hiring another telephone girl," he tells Sam. "Sooner or later, it had to come to this."

"You mean *now?*" Sam asks.

"Now," says Ollie.

SOME QUEUING COMPLICATIONS
AND OTHER CONSIDERATIONS

The example above has probably left you with the impression that waiting-line problems are fairly simple and easy to solve. In some cases they are, and they can be solved with a little imagination and ratiocination. Even here, though, the formulas on page 116 are useful in helping you determine to what extent the arrival or service rates have to be altered to produce a waiting line and waiting time that are a satisfactory solution to the problem. Many problems, however, involve more than one service facility (in either a parallel or series arrangement), as in Joe's barber shop after he hired help, and the formulas that apply are slightly more complicated.

But there are other complications we haven't discussed much: *last-come, first-served disciplines* (such as letters in an "In" box, goods stacked in a warehouse, etc.), *impatient customers* (who may even *add* to delay by complaining about service), *batching problems* (the girls' club that descends on the soda fountain at one time), *unstable queues* (where the service rate is less than the arrival rate and the crowd gets restive—in a delay at a tunnel exit, for example, where they can't leave the line), and other considerations that make the problem so mathematically complex that some other approach toward a solution is sought.

So far, too, we've concerned ourselves with waiting lines where it has been assumed that the potential arrivals are infinite. That is, we assume that there is no limit to the people or work or materials that may arrive for service, while in actual practice many waiting lines are finite. That is, the possible customers who *could* show up for service are limited. For example, in a secretarial pool three secretaries may be available to service 10 managers. When one manager is getting a letter off, the number of managers who might ask for service is down to nine and the number of secretaries available for service is down to two.

Finite waiting lines, as you can imagine, complicate the queuing formulas even more, and the OR analyst may have to turn to finite queuing tables to determine first (in any particular situation) whether the line he is dealing with is to be considered finite or infinite before trying to "solve" the problem. The formulas usually produce results that have to be interpreted in the light of the *measure of effectiveness* (lowest overall cost, minimal customer wait, etc.) previously agreed upon, and this in itself may involve considerable judgment and experience. Finally, arrival rates and service rates must be quantifiable if queuing theory (Q-theory) is to be applied. And if you have inadequate observations (experience) on which to base, say, arrival times—what then? Fortunately, a very ingenious method called "Monte Carlo" has been devised, which is most helpful in simulating chance occurrences if we know their relative frequency. Let's turn now to this helpful, and interesting, technique.

11

MONTE CARLO . . .

How to simulate chance factors in problems you're trying to solve

Monte Carlo, a simulation technique, has proved to be very useful for evaluating the "chance" elements in many OR problems. For example, in a queuing situation the chance arrivals of customers can be simulated through a *random sampling procedure* when the determination of actual arrival times by means of adequate observation may prove to be too expensive, too time-consuming, or otherwise impractical. And the sampling procedure may be used in other situations where the mathematical formulas that apply are too complex to be practical.

Monte Carlo enables you to create an "artificial" model of the situation and to experiment with it until you arrive at a "good enough" solution. It is a means of answering these basic questions: In any given situation, knowing the probability of the variables assuming certain values, what will most likely occur in terms of our measure of effectiveness? If we alter (i.e., change, manipulate, experiment with) the variables, what then will be the results in terms of our measure of effectiveness?

Monte Carlo uses random numbers to simulate chance occurrences, and the problem can then be solved with a pencil (if it is simple enough) or run through a computer thousands of times (if necessary) to experience what would happen over a long period of time. That is, the simulation can be continued to cover as long a period of time as we wish. And the variables can be altered and the simulation repeated as many times as we want, until we feel that we have a solution that is good enough, or about as good as we're likely to get.

To solve problems with Monte Carlo, we need four things: a *measure of effectiveness*, the *relevant variables*, the *cumulative probability distribution* of each variable (i.e., the chance of each of the various values of the variable occurring), and a *set of random numbers*. Tables of such numbers have been prepared by computers and are published in the form of single-digit or multiple-digit columns, each digit of which, because they have been selected at random, has an equal chance of appearing at any place in the entire table. (Figure 11.1 shows such a table.) Of course, you could prepare these tables yourself, using a deck of cards, dice, a roulette wheel, etc.; but if you need thousands of such numbers in solving a problem, creating the tables yourself could be more time-consuming than it's worth.

The first step in using Monte Carlo is to assign random numbers to the various possible values of each variable, so that the probability of the numbers on the chart occurring is equal to the probability of the value of the variable occurring in actual fact. For example, if there is a 25 percent chance of a certain event occurring, then you assign 25 percent of the random numbers to that event (variable value). Using the two-digit chart in Figure 11.1, we can do this by assigning numbers 00 through 24 (25 percent of the total numbers 00 to 99 that appear on the chart) to that particular event (let's call it "A").

Now you are ready to simulate an actual operation. For example,

11 16 43 63 18	75 06 13 76 74	40 60 31 61 52	83 23 53 73 61
21 21 59 17 91	76 83 15 86 78	40 94 15 35 85	69 95 86 09 16
10 43 84 44 82	66 55 83 76 49	73 50 58 34 72	55 95 31 79 57
36 79 22 62 36	33 26 66 65 83	39 41 21 60 13	11 44 28 93 20
73 94 40 47 73	12 03 25 14 14	57 99 47 67 48	54 62 74 85 11
49 56 31 28 72	14 06 39 31 04	61 83 45 91 99	15 46 98 22 85
64 20 84 82 37	41 70 17 31 17	91 40 27 72 ,27	79 51 62 10 07
51 48 67 28 75	38 60 52 93 41	58 29 98 38 80	20 12 51 07 94
99 75 62 63 60	64 51 61 79 71	40 68 49 99 48	33 88 07 64 13
71 32 55 52 17	13 01 57 29 07	75 97 86 42 98	08 07 46 20 55
65 28 59 71 98	12 13 85 30 10	34 55 63 98 61	88 26 77 60 68
17 26 45 73 27	38 22 42 93 01	65 99 05 70 48	25 06 77 75 71
95 63 99 97 54	31 19 99 25 58	16 38 11 50 69	25 41 68 78 75
61 55 57 64 04	86 21 01 18 08	52 45 88 88 80	78 35 26 79 13
78 13 79 87 68	04 68 98 71 30	33 00 78 56 07	92 00 84 48 97
62 49 09 92 15	84 98 72 87 59	38 71 23 15 12	08 58 86 14 90
24 21 66 34 44	21 28 30 70 44	58 72 20 36 78	19 18 66 96 02
16 97 59 54 28	33 22 65 59 03	26 18 86 94 97	51 35 14 77 99
59 13 83 95 42	71 16 85 76 09	12 89 35 40 48	07 25 58 61 49
29 47 85 96 52	50 41 43 19 66	33 18 68 13 46	85 09 53 72 82
96 15 59 50 09	27 42 97 29 18	79 89 32 94 48	88 39 25 42 11
29 62 16 65 83	62 96 61 24 68	48 44 91 51 02	44 12 61 94 38
12 63 97 52 91	71 02 01 72 65	94 20 50 42 59	68 98 35 05 61
14 54 43 71 34	54 71 40 24 01	38 64 80 92 78	81 31 37 74 00
83 40 38 88 27	09 83 41 13 33	04 29 24 60 28	75 66 62 69 54
67 64 20 52 04	30 69 74 48 06	17 02 64 97 37	85 87 51 21 39
64 04 19 90 11	61 04 02 73 09	48 07 07 68 48	02 53 19 77 37
17 04 89 45 23	97 44 45 99 04	30 15 99 54 50	83 77 84 61 15
93 03 98 94 16	52 79 51 06 31	12 14 89 22 31	31 36 16 06 50
82 24 43 43 92	96 60 71 72 20	73 83 87 70 67	24 86 39 75 76
96 99 05 52 44	70 69 32 52 55	73 54 74 37 59	95 63 23 95 55
09 11 97 48 03	97 30 38 87 01	07 27 79 32 17	79 42 12 17 69
57 66 64 12 04	47 58 97 83 64	65 12 84 83 34	07 49 32 80 98
46 49 26 15 94	26 72 95 82 72	38 71 66 13 80	60 21 20 50 99
08 43 31 91 72	08 32 02 08 39	31 92 17 64 58	73 72 00 86 57
10 01 17 50 04	86 05 44 11 90	57 23 82 74 64	61 48 75 23 29
92 42 06 54 31	16 53 00 55 47	24 21 94 10 90	08 53 16 15 78
35 54 25 58 65	07 30 44 70 10	31 30 94 93 87	02 33 00 24 76
86 59 52 62 47	18 55 22 94 91	20 75 09 70 24	72 61 96 66 28
72 11 53 49 85	58 03 69 91 37	28 53 78 43 95	26 65 43 78 51

FIG. 11.1. Random Digits *

* From J. D. Williams, "The Compleat Strategyst: being a primer on the theory of games of strategy," McGraw-Hill Book Company, New York, 1954.

if it is known that 10 events occur each day of your operation, how many times will event A occur on the first day, the second day, etc.? All you have to do is to let the first 10 groups of numbers, reading from left to right on the chart, represent your first day, the second 10 groups of numbers represent your second day, and so on. On the first day, groups of numbers that lie between 00 and 24 occurred five times; on the second day, such groups of numbers occurred only once.

In other words, event A had a 50 percent occurrence on the first day, a 10 percent occurrence on the second day, etc. If you carry this on, the average occurrence will probably be 25 percent, as predicted, but it's the variation from this average during any particular period of operation (e.g., from day to day) that is likely to be significant. This is particularly so when the effectiveness of the system being measured depends upon the relationship among several variables whose values may vary. Perhaps this will become clearer if we use the simple illustration from the chapter on waiting lines to illustrate the simulation of random variables.

MONTE CARLO: JOE'S BARBER SHOP

When Joe first set himself up in business with three chairs, he knew that he would draw most of his business from the 300 families in his area that were located closer to his shop than to any other shop. Each of these families, according to the statistics, consisted of 3.8 members, of whom approximately half were males. He therefore had a potential customer population of 570 men and boys, each of whom, on the average, would get his hair cut every three weeks—or every 15 working days (since Joe's shop was closed on Sundays and Mondays).

If every one of those potential customers used his shop, Joe would have an average of 190 arrivals each week. He figured that he would be able to take care of these, since, working a 48-hour week and averaging 15 minutes to cut each head of hair, he could (at that rate) service 192 customers each week. He expected to reach this maximum within the first year, at which time (at $1.75

a haircut) he would be grossing more than $300 a week—not bad at all. At that point he might consider hiring another barber to help him out, anticipating further growth as a result of planned new-home construction in the area.

Within a few months it was obvious that the barber shop was a going concern. But Joe's success puzzled him. It seemed to him that he had a waiting line half the time, yet he was busy only about 75 percent of the time. It hurt to see people come to the door of the shop, then turn away when they saw the line. But what could he do about it? Even though he was busy only 75 percent of the time himself, if he hired another barber to reduce the waiting time during the 50 percent of the time that it existed, would enough additional customers come into the shop to pay the costs of the added barber?

Joe wasn't a scientist, so his figures were only rough estimates. But he *was* a businessman, and from his cash register tapes he knew that he was servicing approximately 150 customers a week at an average take of $2.10 each (including tips and the charges for additional services, such as shampooing, shave, and massage) and therefore grossing about $315 per week. This naturally pleased him very much . . . but those lost customers bothered him. If he hired an additional barber for $75 a week plus tips (which meant that the return to the shop for each customer serviced by this barber would be $1.85 instead of $2.10), this barber would have to service at least 40 additional customers a week just to pay the cost of his salary. Should Joe do it? At this point . . .

RE-ENTER OLIVER RANDALL

Joe was fortunate in having as his friend a young OR analyst by the name of Oliver Randall (the same). When Joe mentioned the problem, Ollie said that it sounded interesting, but he couldn't afford to give more than a few hours to the problem, and Joe couldn't afford to hire him for the several weeks it would take to do a full-scale study of the situation. "But I'll tell you what I can do," Ollie said. "Maybe I can simulate your operation, using Monte Carlo, and come up with some figures that will be close enough to the truth to tell whether you should hire another man, maybe two, or none at all."

" 'Simulate' I don't know about," replied Joe, "but 'Monte Carlo'? I don't want you to take chances with my business, Ollie."

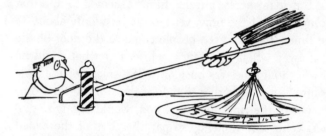

After assuring Joe that he wasn't about to gamble with his business, Ollie had Joe install a one-way mirror in his shop so that Ollie could observe the operation without the necessity of being observed (mistakenly) by arrivals as part of the queue. Over the next several weeks, at various times, he spent spare hours making sample observations of the operation. Finally, when he felt that he had sufficient data from a fairly representative sampling, Ollie tabulated and analyzed them and came up with the following relevant information:

1. To service the average customer took about 15 minutes, but actual service time varied from 7 minutes for a shave only, 15 minutes for a haircut, 22 minutes for a shave and haircut, to 29 minutes for "the works"—shave, haircut, and shampoo. Analyzing his figures, Ollie found that 15 percent of the customers required 7 minutes of service time, 70 percent required 15 minutes, 10 percent required 22 minutes, and 5 percent required the maximum of 29 minutes' service time. The price list for these various services read as follows:

> Shave .... $ .75
> Haircut $1.75
> Shave and Haircut $2.50
> Shave, Haircut, and Shampoo ... $3.50

2. The waiting line, as would be expected, was self-limiting, but Ollie noted the relationship between the length of the line and the number of people who refused to wait, and found that: When the line had one unit (one person), 5 percent of the customers refused to wait; when it had two persons waiting, 20 percent refused to wait; when it consisted of three units, 10 percent refused to wait; when it consisted of four units, 65 percent refused to wait; when it consisted of five units, 95 percent refused to wait; and when there were six people in the line, no customers would wait for service. Adding service units (additional barbers) would, of course, alter this ratio. Ollie had no experience on which to base the ratios that would exist if there were two or three service units, but he found a similar case in the literature on OR and felt that Joe's figures would probably be approximately the same as in this case.

3. While the *average* time between arrivals (including those customers who refused to wait) was about 10 minutes, Ollie found that the pattern of arrivals couldn't be approximated by any of the standard probability distributions. He therefore took enough of a sample to determine the relative frequency of time between arrivals and made up a chart. (See Figure 11.2.)

Time between arrivals, min.	Relative frequency	Random numbers assigned
0	0.11	00-10
2	0.01	11
4	0.06	12-17
6	0.10	18-27
8	0.11	28-38
10	0.22	39-60
12	0.10	61-70
14	0.10	71-80
16	0.08	81-88
18	0.05	89-93
20	0.03	94-96
22	0.02	97-98
24	0.01	99

FIG. 11.2. Arrivals with Random Numbers Assigned

JOE'S BARBER SHOP:
THE PLOT THICKENS

At first glance (or perhaps at the second), it appears that we have enormously complicated the problem. But now, at least, we are in a position to simulate the operation, using a table of random numbers (the one in Figure 11.1, for instance). Of course, we could develop a frequency distribution chart (as we did in the case of Ella in Figure 10.4), but this problem is slightly more complex and we'll need more precise information before deciding to add, or not to add, additional service facilities. Monte Carlo simulation will give us a good idea of what is happening now and what will happen if Joe adds one or two additional barbers.

Our measure of effectiveness in this case is gross profit. The question is: If Joe hires another barber to help him, will this add to, or subtract from, gross profit? The determining factor here, as we have seen, is whether, by adding another barber to the staff, the shop will end up servicing a minimum of 40 additional customers. The relevant variables are the arrival rate and the service rate, both of which vary and both of which determine the length of the waiting line, which in turn determines the number of additional arrivals that join the line during the week.

Waiting line length	One service unit	Random numbers assigned	Two service units	Random numbers assigned	Three service units	Random numbers assigned
1	0.05	00-04	0.03	00-02	0.02	00-01
2	0.20	00-19	0.10	00-09	0.05	00-04
3	0.40	00-39	0.20	00-19	0.10	00-09
4	0.65	00-64	0.35	00-34	0.20	00-19
5	0.95	00-94	0.50	00-49	0.25	00-24
6	1.00	00-99	0.70	00-69	0.35	00-34
7	1.00	00-99	0.95	00-94	0.50	00-49
8	1.00	00-99	1.00	00-99	0.70	00-69
9	1.00	00-99	1.00	00-99	0.95	00-94
10	1.00	00-99	1.00	00-99	1.00	00-99

FIG. 11.3. Relative Frequency Rate of Customers Refusing to Wait

Ollie's sample observations of the operation have provided him with the data he needs to determine the cumulative probability distribution of each variable. All he has to do now is to assign random numbers to the various values of each variable so that the frequency

Service required	Prices of services	Service time required, min	Relative frequency	Random numbers assigned
Shave	$0.75	7	0.15	00-14
Haircut	1.75	15	0.70	15-84
Shave and haircut	2.50	22	0.10	85-94
Shave, haircut, shampoo	3.50	29	0.05	95-99

FIG. 11.4. Service with Random Numbers Assigned

of appearance of the random numbers equals the frequency of appearance of the values. This is easy; and since all the frequencies can be expressed in terms of two-digit numbers, Ollie is going to use a two-digit random number table (Figure 11.1). He therefore makes the assignments shown in Figures 11.2, 11.3, and 11.4.

JOE'S BARBER SHOP: SO LET'S SIMULATE!

Now Ollie is ready to simulate the operation of Joe's barber shop (we're going to do this by hand, although Ollie would probably use a computer, especially in view of the fact that a real problem would be slightly more complicated than this one). The first thing he does is refer to the first number of the random number chart, Figure 11.1 (reading row by row from left to right), to find out when the first chance arrival occurred on the day that he is simulating.

That first number is 11, which means (consulting the list of random numbers assigned to arrivals, Figure 11.2) that customer 1 arrived 2 minutes after the shop opened on that day. With this information, Ollie begins making up the chart shown in Figure 11.5. The first customer, then, arrived at 9:02 and, naturally, there were no customers waiting and no one in Joe's barber chair being serviced. So customer 1 didn't have to wait, and his servicing began the minute he arrived, at 9:02.

What kind of service did he request? Again, Ollie refers to the second number (row 1) on the random digit table (the first number has been used and therefore crossed out). This is a 16, which means (consulting the list of random numbers assigned to services required, Figure 11.4) that customer 1 requests a haircut, which takes 15 minutes. He is therefore finished at 9:17, pays the shop $1.75, and gives Joe a 25-cent tip.

Referring to the random digit table again, Ollie finds that the second customer arrived at 9:12 after an interval of 10 minutes and, because customer 1 was still in the chair, had to wait 5 minutes for service. He waited because there was no waiting line. Thus Ollie continues to make up his chart of the day's operations, determining customer arrivals, whether they wait or not, and service required, by consulting the random digit table and the assignments made according to the frequency rates in Figure 11.4.

Finally, when customer 4 arrives, he finds a waiting line of one person (customer 3). Will he wait, or go away? To find out, Ollie refers to the next number (the eighth in row 1) on the random number chart, which is a 13. Consulting the random numbers assigned to people who do not wait when there is a line (Figure 11.3), Ollie finds (in the third column, first row, next to "One service unit," waiting line of one) that he would have to be one of the numbers 00 to 04 not to wait; customer 4 therefore waits.

Ollie continues through the day this way, consulting the random number chart and the assignments he has made to answer these three questions about each customer: When does he arrive? Will he wait (if there is a line)? and What service does he require? And Ollie finds that Joe is running a pretty tight little operation—but that he is overly concerned about people not waiting. Only nine arrivals fail to join the line (which means that Joe lost only 9 × approximately $2.10, or $18.90). What's more, the line never got longer than four people waiting at any one time, and the longest wait for any of his customers was 66 minutes—which was just about the time he began to lose customers. And Joe had no idle time all day. It was obvious to Ollie that Joe's operation was quite efficient

Customer	Arrival interval, min	Time of arrival	Customer being serviced	Customers waiting	Wait yes	Wait no	Length of wait, min	When serviced	Service time, min	When finished	Payment	Tip
1	2	9:02	....	....	x		0	9:02	15	9:17	$1.75	$0.25
2	10	9:12	1	....	x		5	9:17	15	9:32	1.75	0.25
3	6	9:18	2	....	x		14	9:32	15	9:47	1.75	0.25
4	0	9:18	2	3	x		29	9:47	15	10:02	1.75	0.25
5	14	9:32	3	4	x		30	10:02	15	10:17	1.75	0.25
6	8	9:40	3	4,5	x		37	10:17	15	10:32	1.75	0.25
7	16	9:56	4	5,6	x		36	10:32	15	10:47	1.75	0.25
8	14	10:10	5	6,7	x		37	10:47	15	11:02	1.75	0.25
9	6	10:16	5	6,7,8	x		46	11:02	15	11:17	1.75	0.25
10	18	10:34	7	8,9	x		43	11:17	15	11:32	1.75	0.25
11	4	10:38	7	8,9,10	x		54	11:32	15	11:47	1.75	0.25
12	10	10:48	8	9,10,11	x		59	11:47	15	12:02	1.75	0.25
13	8	10:56	8	9,10,11, 12	x		66	12:02	15	12:17	1.75	0.25
14	20	11:16	9	10,11,12, 13	x		61	12:17	7	12:24	0.75	0.10
15	4	11:20	10	11,12,13, 14		x						
16	10	11:40	11	12,13,14	x		44	12:24	15	12:39	1.75	0.25
17	16	11:56	12	13,14,16	x		43	12:39	15	12:54	1.75	0.25
18	16	12:12	13	14,16,17	x		42	12:54	15	1:09	1.75	0.25
19	14	12:26	16	17,18	x		43	1:09	15	1:24	1.75	0.25
20	8	12:34	16	17,18,19	x		50	1:24	15	1:39	1.75	0.25
21	20	12:54	18	19,20	x		45	1:39	15	1:54	1.75	0.25
22	10	1:04	18	19,20,21		x						
23	14	1:18	19	20,21	x		36	1:54	15	2:09	1.75	0.25
24	8	1:26	20	21,23	x		43	2:09	15	2:24	1.75	0.25
25	12	1:38	20	21,23,24	x		46	2:24	15	2:39	1.75	0.25
26	10	1:48	21	23,24,25	x		51	2:39	15	2:54	1.75	0.25
27	10	1:58	23	24,25,26		x						
28	2	2:00	23	24,25,26	x		54	2:54	15	3:09	1.75	0.25
29	18	2:18	24	25,26,28		x						
30	14	2:32	25	26,28	x		37	3:09	15	3:24	1.75	0.25
31	10	2:42	26	28,30	x		42	3:24	7	3:31	0.75	0.10
32	0	2:42	26	28,30,31		x						
33	4	2:46	26	28,30,31		x						
34	10	2:56	28	30,31	x		35	3:31	15	3:46	1.75	0.25
35	12	3:08	28	30,31,34	x		38	3:46	15	4:01	1.75	0.25
36	12	3:20	30	31,34,35	x		41	4:01	22	4:23	2.50	0.30
37	2	3:22	30	31,34,35, 36		x						
38	10	3:32	34	35,36	x		51	4:23	15	4:38	1.75	0.25
39	14	3:46	35	36,38	t	x						
40	0	3:46	35	36,38		x						
41	8	3:54	35	36,38		x						
42	12	4:06	36	38	x		32	4:38	15	4:53	1.75	0.25
43	18	4:24	38	42	x		29	4:53	15	5:08	1.75	0.25
44	10	4:34	38	42,43	x		34	5:08	15	5:23	1.75	0.25
45	16	4:50	42	43,44	x		33	5:23	15	5:38	1.75	0.25

Customer 46 arrived at 5:06 and found the door locked for the day.

Totals $60.00 $8.50

Gross $68.50

FIG. 11.5. Monte Carlo Simulation (One Day, One Service Unit)

(though he simulated several weeks of operation just to be sure), and that he would only lose money (at least initially and for an indeterminate period) by hiring a second barber.

Joe was very pleased with Ollie's report, but by the end of another six months he began to get very disturbed again. He was busier than ever, he seemed to always have more people waiting, and he knew that he was losing many customers—and it wasn't just his imagination. "Maybe the time has come to hire that second barber," he figured, and he asked Ollie to do another study for him.

Time between arrivals, min	Relative frequency	Random numbers assigned
0	0.12	00-11
1	0.03	12-14
2	0.02	15-16
3	0.04	17-20
4	0.05	21-25
5	0.05	26-30
6	0.06	31-36
7	0.07	37-43
8	0.08	44-51
9	0.09	52-60
10	0.12	61-72
11	0.10	73-82
12	0.09	83-91
13	0.05	92-96
14	0.03	97-99

FIG. 11.6.   Arrivals of Customers

Ollie was glad to oblige, and the first thing he did was to sample the operation again. Everything, he found, was the same, except that Joe was right about the customer arrivals: there were more of them (meaning that the time between arrivals was considerably shorter) and the waiting lines were longer. He therefore drew up a chart (Figure 11.6) of arrival intervals and their relative frequency and assigned random numbers to them again, and he was in business.

With this new chart, Ollie simulated the operation of Joe's barber shop once again—but this time with *two* barbers (two service units).

Customer	Arrival interval, min	Time of arrival	Customers waiting	Customers serviced		Wait		Length of wait, min	When serviced	Service time, min	When finished	Payment	Tip	
				1	2	Yes	No						1	2
1	11	9:11	....	0	0	x		0	9:11	15	9:26	$1.75	$0.25	
2	7	9:18	....	1	0	x		0	9:18	15	9:33	1.75		0.25
3	3	9:21	....	1	2	x		5	9:26	15	9:41	1.75	0.25	
4	3	9:24	. 3	1	2	x		9	9:33	15	9:48	1.75		0.25
5	5	9:29	4	3	2	x		12	9:41	15	9:56	1.75	0.25	
6	11	9:40	5	3	4	x		8	9:48	15	10:03	1.75		0.25
7	0	9:40	6,5	3	4		x	--						
8	8	9:48	....	5	6	x		8	9:56	15	10:11	1.75	0.25	
9	10	9:58	....	8	6	x		5	10:03	15	10:18	1.75		0.25
10	11	10:09	....	8	9	x		2	10:11	15	10:26	1.75	0.25	
11	9	10:18	....	10	--	x		0	10:18	15	10:33	1.75		0.25
12	13	10:31	....	--	11	x		0	10:31	15	10:46	1.75	0.25	
13	9	10:40	....	12	--	x		0	10:40	15	10:55	1.75		0.25
14	14	10:54	....	--	13	x		0	10:54	15	11:09	1.75	0.25	
15	11	11:05	....	14	--	x		0	11:05	15	11:20	1.75		0.25
16	1	11:06	....	14	15	x		3	11:09	15	11:24	1.75	0.25	
17	0	11:06	16	14	15	x		14	11:20	29	11:49	3.50		0.50
18	11	11:17	17	16	15	x		7	11:24	15	11:39	1.75	0.25	
19	9	11:26	....	18	17	x		13	11:39	15	11:54	1.75	0.25	
20	8	11:34	19	18	17	x		15	11:49	15	12:04	1.75		0.25
21	10	11:44	20,19	18	17	x		10	11:54	15	12:09	1.75	0.25	
22	8	11:52	21	19	20	x		12	12:04	15	12:19	1.75	0.25	
23	6	11:58	22	21	20	x		11	12:09	7	12:16	0.75		0.10
24	10	12:08	23	21	22		x	--	--	--	--	--		
25	10	12:18	....	--	22	x		0	12:18	15	12:33	1.75	0.25	
26	9	12:27	....	25	--	x		0	12:27	15	12:42	1.75		0.25
27	3	12:30	....	25	26	x		3	12:33	7	12:40	0.75	0.10	
28	0	12:30	27	25	26	x		10	12:40	15	12:55	1.75	0.25	
29	0	12:30	28,27	25	26	x		12	12:42	29	1:01	3.50		0.50
30	12	12:42	....	28	29	x		13	12:55	15	1:10	1.75	0.25	
31	14	12:56	....	30	29	x		5	1:01	7	1:08	0.75		0.10
32	0	12:56	31	30	29	x		12	1:08	15	1:23	1.75		0.25
33	9	1:05	32	30	31	x		5	1:10	15	1:25	1.75	0.25	
34	9	1:14	33	33	32	x		9	1:23	15	1:38	1.75		0.25
35	14	1:28	....	--	34	x		0	1:28	7	1:35	0.75	0.10	
36	1	1:29	....	35	34	x		6	1:35	22	1:57	2.50	0.30	
37	5	1:34	36	35	34	x		4	1:38	15	1:53	1.75		0.25
38	9	1:43	....	36	37	x		10	1:53	15	2:08	1.75		0.25
39	14	1:57	....	--	38	x		0	1:57	15	2:12	1.75	0.25	
40	12	2:09	....	39	--	x		0	2:09	15	2:24	1.75		0.25
41	11	2:20	....	--	40	x		0	2:20	15	2:35	1.75	0.25	
42	10	2:30	....	41	--	x		0	2:30	15	2:45	1.75		0.25
43	5	2:35	....	--	42	x		0	2:35	15	2:50	1.75	0.25	
44	11	2:46	....	43	--	x		0	2:46	15	3:01	1.75		0.25
45	7	2:53	....	--	44	x		0	2:53	15	3:08	1.75	0.25	
46	7	3:00	....	45	44	x		1	3:01	22	3:23	2.50		0.30
47	0	3:00	46	45	44	x		8	3:08	29	3:37	3.50	0.50	
48	0	3:00	47,46	45	44	x		23	3:23	15	3:38	1.75		0.25
49	4	3:04	48,47	45	46		x	--	--	--	--	--		
50	11	3:15	48	47	46	x		22	3:37	15	3:52	1.75	0.25	
51	13	3:28	50	47	48	x		10	3:38	29	4:07	3.50		0.50
52	14	3:42	....	50	51	x		10	3:52	15	4:07	1.75	0.25	
53	6	3:48	52	50	51	x		19	4:07	29	4:36	3.50		0.50
54	4	3:52	53	52	51	x		15	4:07	15	4:22	1.75	0.25	
55	7	3:59	54,53	52	51	x		23	4:22	15	4:37	1.75	0.25	
56	10	4:09	55	54	53	x		27	4:36	15	4:51	1.75		0.25
57	10	4:19	56,55	54	53	x		18	4:37	15	4:52	1.75	0.25	
58	10	4:29	57,56	55	53	x		22	4:51	15	5:13	1.75		0.25
59	10	4:39	58	57	56	x		13	4:52	22	5:14	2.50	0.30	
60	4	4:43	59,58	57	56		x	--	--	--	--	--		
61	3	4:46	59,58	57	56		x	--	--	--	--	--		
62	9	4:54	....	59	58	x		19	5:13	15	5:28	1.75		0.25

Customer 63 arrived at 5:06 and found the doors closed for the day.   Totals $106.75 $7.55 $7.40

Joe's gross (minus 2's salary of $15) = $99.30

FIG. 11.7. Monte Carlo Simulation (One Day, Two Service Units)

Starting with the fourth number in the seventh row of his random number table (he had used up all the numbers preceding this one in his previous simulation), he found that the first customer arrived after an 11-minute interval at 9:11 (the first number on the chart was 82, which on the new assignment chart for arrivals meant an 11-minute interval). Of course, when waiting lines developed, as they did in the afternoon, Ollie used the random numbers assigned to the waiting-line length under a "Two service units" operation to determine whether that particular arrival waited or not.

Ollie was pleased to report to Joe that, yes, he definitely could use a second barber. According to his simulation (which he confirmed with additional simulations), Joe would ring up a total of $106.75 with a two-man operation on a typical day. Out of this he would have to pay the man's salary of $15 for the day (the man's tips of $7.40 were his own, of course); but even so, after doing this and figuring in his own tips of $7.55, he would gross $99.30—a substantial hike over the $68.50 he grossed under the original one-man simulation.

12

WHEN IS ENOUGH ENOUGH? . . .

How to decide when and how much to order of what

Practically speaking, an inventory is a supply of anything that is being held for ultimate use or sale. Books in a library are inventory. Animals on a game farm waiting to be sold and shipped to zoos are inventory. A store of parts waiting to be used in a finished product is inventory. Even the supply of razor blades in your medicine cabinet is inventory. In fact, a consideration of this last problem could be quite instructive.

How many razor blades should you purchase at one time? When should you reorder? To answer, of course, we'd have to know the rate of use, the cost of storage (not just the cost of space, but the loss of interest on the capital invested), the discounts involved in quantity purchases, the probability of the costs of blades going up or down during the ordering interval, costs connected with the purchase (time, gas, etc.), and some measure of the inconvenience of running out or using a dull blade.

If the question of razor blades in your medicine cabinet seems frivolous, it's because the dollar amounts involved are likely to be inconsequential and because, when the word "inventory" is used, we tend to think of goods on a retailer's shelf, stock in a manufacturer's warehouse, or a supply of items we intend to utilize in production. Here the amounts involved can be quite consequential and the problems quite complicated.

INVENTORY AND ITS COSTS

As with a queue, we usually have an inventory when it costs less to *have* an inventory than *not* to have an inventory. In other words, an inventory saves you money and is an investment with a definite return which can be calculated. Your objective should be to maximize the return on that investment, and not necessarily to minimize costs. After all, in a narrow sense, the inventory that costs the least is the inventory that doesn't exist. But it's the rare system that can exist without one.

This chapter will be concerned with three kinds of costs that make up what we shall call the "total" cost of inventory: the costs of carrying *surplus* inventory, the costs of a *shortage*, and *setup* (or ordering) costs. *Surplus* costs are the costs of carrying more inventory than you have to. *Shortage* costs are the costs (loss of profits, production delays, downtime, etc.) of being out of a part or product when it is needed for sale or use. *Setup* costs are the costs of setting up for a production run of, or ordering, a certain quantity of inventory to fill an anticipated need.

There are other costs that we shall *not* concern ourselves with. For example, you may be able to reduce your inventory costs by building a warehouse instead of renting warehouse space, or by moving a supply depot out of the city into the suburbs, or by rearranging the physical layout of your plant or office. Instead, we shall assume that considerations like these have been examined beforehand. Our problem is simply this: Given the conditions that prevail (cost of space, cost of goods, cost of ordering, etc.), and particularly in view of supply and demand, what inventory level should we maintain? How often should we order, and in what quantities? Let's take this last question first.

HOW MUCH AND WHEN

In its simplest form, the problem of how much to order and when has three parameters (given conditions, limiting factors, etc.): the rate at which the inventory is being used (or anticipated usage), symbolized by r, storage costs (C_s), and setup or preparation costs (C_p). If we know these values, then we can determine the most economical ordering quantity (EOQ), or optimum quantity (Q_o), using a variation of an equation first developed by F. W. Harris in 1915 and called the "lot size," or "square root," formula: *

$$Q_o = \sqrt{\frac{2rC_p}{C_s}}$$

Translated into English, this equation says that "optimum quantity equals the square root of 2 times the rate of usage (r) times

* The justification for the formula is that it maximizes profit by minimizing costs. However, most contemporary inventory problems are more complicated than this formula would seem to suggest, and if used it can result in serious production difficulties in some circumstances, or in inflated inventory levels. In other words, this formula assumes simplicity and predictability of the inventory situation, characteristics which are largely nonexistent. However, it will do for illustrative purposes.

setup costs (C_p) divided by storage costs (C_s)." To make this clearer, let's imagine a small stationery store handling a product that doesn't obsolesce (i.e., lose its value), for which there is a demand of 4,000 units each year. If it costs the stationer 10 cents per unit to store the product on an annual basis (cost of space, insurance, etc.), and $2.00 to order it (paperwork, postage, etc.) regardless of the size of the order, he may well want to know how often he should order and in what quantity. The lot size formula tells him:

$$Q_o = \sqrt{\frac{2 \times 4,000 \times 2.00}{0.10}} = 400 \text{ units}$$

In other words, the stationer should order 400 units at a time, since this is the most economical ordering quantity.

Yes, but *when* should he place this order? Well, since he orders 400 units at a time, and the rate of usage is 4,000 units per year, this means that he will have to place an order 10 times a year (4,000 divided by 400) if he is to meet the demand. And dividing 365 (days in the year) by 10 gives $36\frac{1}{2}$, which means that he should place the order every $36\frac{1}{2}$ days, assuming that the demand is even and that shortages are not to be permitted.

Yes, but *when* should he place the order—i.e., when the inventory level is at what point? If delivery is immediate, there is no problem: he simply orders 400 additional units whenever he sells the last unit in stock. In this case, his inventory level, charted,

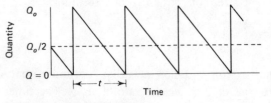

FIG. 12.1.   Inventory Level

will follow the classic pattern in Figure 12.1, where inventory is depleted at a constant rate from $Q_o = 400$ to $Q = 0$ over a period of time ($t = 36\frac{1}{2}$ days), and the average inventory will therefore be Q_o divided by 2. Total inventory costs can be determined by the formula $(Q_o/2)C_s + NC_p$, where N = number of orders. In this case, total inventory costs will equal $(200 \times \$.10) + (10 \times \$2.00)$, or $40 per year.

DELVING A LITTLE DEEPER

That inventory problems are likely to be a little more complex than this is obvious. In the first place, delivery is seldom immediate. It may take hours, days, or years (even a half-century or more in the case of a paper products company waiting for seedlings to mature into timber) for delivery to be completed. Of course, if this time lag is known with certainty, it poses no problem. You simply work back from the date at which inventory (Q) equals zero to determine your reorder point. If delivery takes a week, for example, then you place your order a week before the date on which $Q = 0$.

The important thing to remember is that the reorder point (assuming that the rate of usage is constant) is based on *time*, not on quantity or inventory level, which is contrary to established practice in many companies. If inventory is depleted at a constant rate (as in Figure 12.1), you can draw a perpendicular line from the time scale to determine the inventory level at which the new order should be placed. But if the rate of usage is variable (a problem we shall get into shortly), then the probability of demand during the ordering period has to be determined and used to work back along the level-of-inventory line to find that particular value of Q at which a new order should be placed.

The trouble with this kind of figuring is that delivery is seldom 100 percent certain. The uncertainty of supply, the possibility of

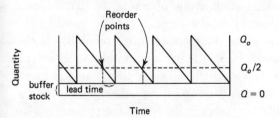

FIG. 12.2.   Inventory Level with Buffer Stock

a breakdown in transportation, etc., make it probable that the ordering period may exceed its expected length. What, then, is an executive who is concerned with inventories to do? He solves this problem by maintaining what is known as a *buffer*, or safety, stock. Our classical inventory model now begins to look like that in Figure 12.2.

How is the amount of buffer stock to be determined? One common method, if the costs of a shortage are intolerable, is to simply estimate the longest delay that can possibly occur and maintain a buffer stock equivalent to the demand that is likely to occur during this period. But if shortage costs are reasonable enough to bear, and the probability of delay in delivery is very small, then you may want little or no buffer stock. The *exact* amount to maintain in most situations lies somewhere between these two points and is determined by balancing shortage costs against surplus costs in the light of the probability of delay for the time period concerned.

BUT SUPPOSE DEMAND VARIES?

The question of how much to order and when is further complicated when demand varies from ordering period to ordering period. In the case of the stationery store owner, for example, suppose that 400 units is only the *average* demand during an ordering period of 36½ days? Theoretically, the demand can vary from zero to infinity, although in the past demand has averaged 400 units, plus or minus 100 units, each ordering period. The temptation in many such cases is to say, "To hell with all this fancy figuring. If I have excess inventory at the end of my ordering period, or a shortage, I'll just decrease or increase my next order accordingly."

The fallacy in this kind of thinking, of course, is that it means basing the ordering quantity on the demand that occurred in the *last* time period instead of on the more realistic probability of the demand in the next period. It's a little like a man walking backward, or a man driving a car who overreacts to every little bump or curve in the road so that he swerves back and forth before getting the car straight once again. His inventory is likely to take the same wide (and in this case, uneconomical) swings. For example . . .

Suppose that the stationery store owner has excess inventory of 100 units at the end of an ordering period. Following the thinking above, he places an order for 300 units to bring his inventory back up to 400. But during the next time period, the demand equals 500 units. The owner therefore loses the profit on 100 units. And because he was 100 units short, he orders 500 units. But when the demand over the next period falls to 300, he is stuck with excess inventory of 200 units. He therefore only orders 200 units, etc., etc. And so it goes, with the owner losing money left and right through excessive surplus, shortage, and setup costs.

Automatically ordering a set quantity when the inventory reaches a certain level may seem like a better approach—and in many cases it *can* provide a "good enough" solution. Especially when little in dollar value is involved, a little oversupply can be cheap enough insurance. For example, the "bin approach" can be useful in maintaining a small supply of bolts and nuts for use within a department. The idea is to keep two bins of the item needed, and when one is empty to automatically order another supply, assuming that there is sufficient inventory in one bin to meet the demand during the delivery period. But in most cases the situation is a little more complicated than this, and the costs involved can be very large or even infinite (i.e., they can result in the failure of the business).

Before we go on to show how to determine the optimum inventory level, which by definition is that inventory which is likely to cost you the least to maintain in the total sense and in terms of your overall company objectives, we might do well to take a look at the function of inventories.

THE FUNCTION OF INVENTORY

At the beginning of this chapter, we said that an inventory is a supply of something being held for ultimate use or sale—which is correct. But it will be more helpful, perhaps, to view inventory as a *system,* a system that can be programmed and determined by models (mathematical equations, for the most part). This system is made up of three components—input, storage, and output (i.e., stock coming into the system, stock being held, and stock being released from the system). At one end of this system you have supply, and at the other end you have demand. In fact, inventory can be defined as something that comes between supply and demand whose function is to decouple them (i.e., to lessen the immediacy with which one is dependent upon the other).

In a very real sense, each unit of inventory represents the purchase of a unit of time. And we need inventory primarily because of the factor called *time lag*. In other words, sometimes supply lags behind demand, sometimes demand lags behind supply. If supply always equaled demand, there would be no need for inventories—that is, if we could supply immediately what was demanded (and if there were no setup costs). Such systems, of course, already exist. One of these is your electricity supply. The supply always equals demand, you pay only for what you use, and there are no ordering costs. Another is your gas supply, if you use natural gas to heat your home.

But if you still use coal to heat your home, or remember what it was like to use coal, you can appreciate the need for inventory, and many of the problems involved. Without inventory, every time you needed a bucket of coal for the furnace, you would have to call your supplier and have him deliver it immediately. Thus you would be terribly dependent upon him—and he on you, since you might call at any time of the night or day and if he didn't respond immediately he would lose your business. But by maintaining an inventory of coal in the coal bin in the cellar you lessen the immediacy of that dependency. For as long as it exists, that inventory has decoupled supply and demand. The supply of coal in the cellar represents the purchase of time (a few weeks, a few months) before you will have to go back to that source again for the satisfaction of your needs.

THE FUNCTION OF INVENTORY (CONTINUED)

In a sense, then, inventory represents delivery time, production time, etc.—the time it takes to produce and/or deliver units of inventory from the moment the order is placed to the moment of receipt. But inventory also has other functions, two of which are of major importance. One of these is to reduce setup costs (costs of ordering, shipping, setting up production, etc.) by making larger orders, shipments, and production runs possible. The other is to insure the system against the losses (sometimes enormous) associated with shortages or delays. Which of the two is more important depends upon the particular inventory under discussion.

Most inventory systems, as we have said, involve input, storage, and output. Stock in a normal system will therefore be found at the beginning of the system as part of the input inventory (e.g., as raw material or parts), in transit through the system (e.g., as part of the production process), and at the end of the system as output inventory (e.g., as finished goods). These different inventories exist for the same basic reasons (i.e., have the same functions), but the emphasis in each case will vary somewhat (as, indeed, it might from company to company). For example:

- The primary function of *input inventories* (raw materials, parts, finished products, etc., waiting to be used) is to insure against uncertain supply or uncertain delivery, to reduce ordering costs, and to take advantage of price breaks (e.g., quantity discounts).

- The primary function of *transit inventories* (semifinished products, parts, etc., tied up in the production process) is to ensure smooth production, to avoid production delays, to take into account the fact that there may be variations in the production capacities of different men, machines, departments, etc. (Frequently the inventories for different machines or departments can be determined separately and form inventory systems within the overall inventory system.)

- The primary function of *output inventories* (finished goods, parts, etc., waiting to be sold or shipped out), of course, is to allow for fluctuations in demand. In the grossest sense, for example, you may have a seasonal demand but find it most economical to manufacture on a year-round basis, building inventories to allow for the variations in demand.

But whatever your inventory problem, whatever the costs or factors involved, it will usually boil down to the question we have been considering (how much to order and when) and/or the question we are about to consider: What inventory level should we maintain—that is, what inventory level will be optimum in terms of our objectives (usually, least cost)? To answer it, we shall turn now to a relatively simple example, that of a newspaper boy who wants to know how many newspapers he should order each day (what inventory level he should maintain) to maximize his earnings in the face of fluctuating demand.

THE CASE OF RAGGEDY DICK

Dick, the newspaper boy, sells an average of 10 newspapers a day. He pays 5 cents for each newspaper he orders and sells it for 10 cents. Knowing only this, we would assume that he makes an average profit of 50 cents each day. But Dick has a problem: demand fluctuates. He may sell 5 papers one day and 15 the next. And if he orders too many newspapers and has to return any of them to the supplier, he is paid only 1 cent for each newspaper returned. The problem is: how many newspapers should Dick order each day (i.e., what inventory should he maintain), in view of the fluctuating demand, to maximize his profits?

Since the setup costs in this problem are virtually nil (all Dick has to do on the rare occasions when he wants to change his order, or inventory level, is to place a 10-cent phone call), it boils down to a question of too much versus too little—that is, of balancing surplus costs against shortage costs so that total costs are minimal and hence profits are maximum.

At first glance, if we assume that the average demand is for 10 newspapers each day, the common-sense solution to the problem might be to start each day with 10 newspapers to meet that average demand. But two considerations immediately come to mind. First, fluctuations in demand below 10 will result in average sales of *less* than 10. Second, since shortage costs are higher than surplus costs (5 cents per newspaper as compared to 4 cents per newspaper), wouldn't it be better to err on the side of excess inventory?

Since both of the above considerations seem to make sense, let's start Dick out with an initial inventory of 11 newspapers each day. If the demand one day is for 5 newspapers and the next 15, then Dick makes 1 cent the first day (25 cents profit on 5 newspapers sold minus a 24-cent loss on 6 newspapers not sold) and 55 cents the second day (the profit on 11 newspapers sold), for an average daily profit of 28 cents—a far cry from the 50 cents we assumed he would make each day. In addition to this, he had shortage costs on the second day of 20 cents (the loss on 4 newspapers not sold). Is 11 his optimum inventory? We don't know. But shortage and surplus costs that average 22 cents a day seem rather high.

Of course, by experimenting with his inventory level and keeping one eye on profit and loss, Dick (and most firms, for that matter) can eventually arrive at the inventory level that returns the most profit. But experimentation when you're dealing with thousands of dollars instead of pennies can be quite costly, particularly in a situation like Dick's, where there is a wide fluctuation in a demand that follows no predictable pattern.

It's the function of OR, and of the scientific approach in general, to help avoid that cost; and Dick, if he's hep to scientific decision-making, will recognize the fact that he has a problem that can be solved by OR. Whether he should actually call in an analyst to work on the problem is something else; but since we're offering our services for free, what has he got to lose? Let's therefore, take . . .

AN OR APPROACH TO THE CASE OF RAGGEDY DICK

The first step in any kind of rational approach to decision-making is always to ask, What is our problem? In this case, it's to determine Dick's optimum inventory level (I_o), expressed as the number of newspapers he should order each day to maximize his profits (N). What do we know? We know that each paper sold (s) has the value of 10 cents, that each paper Dick buys (b) costs 5 cents, and that Dick receives 1 cent (r) for each paper returned. Beyond these given values, this is essentially a problem with a single parameter: *the average demand equals* 10. But the average doesn't tell us how many papers will be demanded on any given day. Theoretically, the demand (n) can vary from 0 to infinity. To solve our problem, the first thing we have to do is to determine the probability (P) of n occurring. Fortunately, help is available.

In cases like this, where n is potentially large (or infinite) and P is small, and the product nP remains relatively constant; then $P(n)$ will assume what is known as a Poisson distribution * if charted. That is, it will form a definite pattern, and the value of $P(n)$ can be determined. The values of $P(n)$ for various means have been worked out and are available in Poisson distribution charts.

Figure 12.3, for example, shows the probability (P) of n (demand) occurring at values from 0 to infinity when the average demand is 10. The third column gives the accumulated value

$$\left(\sum_{i=0}^{n}\right) P_i(n) \qquad \text{of } P(n), \text{ from } i = 0 \text{ through the range of } n,$$

where I is a dummy variable. For example, the accumulated value of $P(n)$ from $i = 0$ to $n = 16$

$$\left(\sum_{i=0}^{n=16} P(n)\right) \qquad \text{is 0.973—which is to say, "When average de-}$$

mand equals 10, the chance of n assuming a value from 0 to 16 is 973 out of a thousand." However, the chance of n assuming the

---

* Observations that assume a (binomial) distribution are based upon a sample of definite size; hence n is known and therefore finite. In such cases we know how many times the event *did* occur and how many times it did *not* occur. But in the case of observations that assume a Poisson distribution, the sample size is unknown and therefore potentially large or infinite. We don't know how many times the event did not occur, only how many times it did, over a certain period of time. The number of lightning flashes that occur during a half-hour period is an example of the latter. The number of men with an IQ of 100 out of a sample of 1,000 would be an example of the former.

n (number of newspapers demanded)	$P(n)$ (probability of demand occurring)	$\sum_{i=0}^{n} P_i(n)$ (accumulated probability of demand)
0	0.000	0.000
1	0.000	0.000
2	0.003	0.003
3	0.007	0.010
4	0.019	0.029
5	0.038	0.067
6	0.063	0.130
7	0.090	0.220
8	0.113	0.333
9	0.125	0.458
10	0.125	0.583
11	0.114	0.697
12	0.095	0.792
13	0.072	0.864
14	0.053	0.917
15	0.034	0.951
16	0.022	0.973
17	0.013	0.986
18	0.007	0.993
19	0.004	0.997
20	0.001	0.998
21	0.001	0.999
22	0.001	1.000
23	0.000	1.000
∞	0.000	1.000

FIG. 12.3. Poisson Distribution Chart for Mean of 10

value of exactly 16, say, is only 0.022, according to the chart in Figure 12.3.

DETERMINING THE OPTIMUM INVENTORY

By examining the chart, we can see that Dick's optimum inventory will lie somewhere in the range of 2 through 22, since the chance of the demand being less than 2 or more than 22 is nil. The net profit (N) Dick can expect from any of these values of I (inventory) will be total revenue (R) less total cost (C) or $N(I) = R(I) - C(I)$.

It would be nice if we could work with a model as simple as this, but unfortunately, while $C(I)$ will always equal bI (cost of the individual paper times each number ordered), the value of $R(I)$ will depend on whether it includes returns (r) and how many. When demand is equal to or greater than inventory, $R(I)$ will have the value of sI (selling price times number sold), since there will be no returns. But when demand is less than inventory, $R(I)$ will equal $sn + r(I - n)$. Therefore, our model has to include *both* values of $R(I)$ to be accurate: $sn + r(I - n)$ for all values of $R(I)$ from $n = 0$ to $n = I - 1$, plus sI for all values of $R(I)$ from $n = 1$ to $n =$ maximum. Our completed model of this particular problem situation now looks like this:

$$N(I) = \sum_{n=0}^{n=I-1} [sn + r(I - n)]P(n) + sIP \sum_{n=I}^{n=n\max} (n) - bI$$

We could, if we wanted to, solve our problem with this model by determining the value of N for all values of I from 2 through 22 (our theoretical limits), varying n in each case from 2 through 22. But this could be quite tedious, since it would involve computing the value of N 21 times for each of 21 values of I, a total of 441 computations, before we could be sure which level of inventory is likely to be optimum. Instead, let's see if we can't find a shortcut to the answer of optimum inventory by using a little logic and manipulating the symbols.

SHORTCUT TO SUCCESS

First of all, we know that, since the demand averages 10 papers a day and Dick makes 5 cents per paper, the theoretical maximum profit (N) is 50 cents. This would be the case if the inventory equaled the demand each day. But since demand fluctuates, we can only hope to determine an inventory that will optimize N. The optimum inventory (I_o) is by definition that inventory where $N(I_o) \geqq N(I_o - 1)$ and $N(I_o) \leqq N(I_o + 1)$. In other words, if you add to or take away from the optimum inventory, you cannot hope to increase profit and (in all likelihood) will decrease it.

It also doesn't take long to figure out that, since shortage costs exceed surplus costs, we might do better to err on the side of excessive inventory if we are going to err at all. In other words, excess inventory produces a revenue that insufficient inventory doesn't, and this should be a factor in determining our optimum inventory level. Therefore, we can theoretically achieve maximum profit by maintaining an inventory slightly in excess of demand. But how much in excess? This can be determined in a crude way by multiplying

$$\frac{s - b}{b - r} \times n = \frac{0.05}{0.04} \times n, \qquad \text{where } n \text{ is the average of the de-}$$

mand. Using this rough formula, Dick's optimum inventory would be 12.5.)

However, this formula, as well as the inventory rate stated on page 139, should be considered as rules of thumb to be applied to inventory problems of minor monetary consequence. The accuracy of the inventory calculation can be improved by taking into consideration the fact that while excess inventory produces r, it (like a shortage) involves a loss (-4 cents in this case) of a profit that *might have been made* if n equaled I. In other words, if shortage costs equal $s - b$, then surplus costs equal $s - b$ plus $b - r$, or $s - r$. We are now in a position to construct a model of great significance, one that will provide the shortcut we need. In fact, in a simple case such as Dick's, where our only concern is the question of too much versus too little, the relationship between shortage costs and surplus costs, as expressed in the model $(s - b)/(s - r)$, gives us the exact value of

$$\sum_{n=0}^{n=I_o} P(n) \qquad \text{which we need.}$$

By referring to the particular Poisson distribution chart for the average demand we are concerned with, we can readily determine the value of I_o that comes closest to satisfying this formula. In Dick's case,

$$\frac{s-b}{s-r}=\frac{0.05}{0.09}=0.556;$$ therefore that inventory is optimum

which satisfies *both* these equations (which derive from our definition of I_o on page 150):

$$\sum_{n=0}^{n=I_o-1}P(n)\leqq 0.556 \quad \text{and} \quad \sum_{n=0}^{n=I_o}P(n)\geqq 0.556.$$ A check

of the chart in Figure 12.3 shows that the only value of I_o that satisfies *both* these equations is 10 (the accumulated value of $n=10-1$ is 0.458, which is equal to or less than 0.556; and the accumulated value of $n=10$ is 0.583, which is equal to or greater than 0.556). So 10 is the solution to Dick's problem.

Of course, this still doesn't tell us how much Dick can hope to

$n=2$	$0.10 \times 2 + 0.01$ (10-2) $0.003 =$	0.00084
$n=3$	$0.10 \times 3 + 0.01$ (10-3) $0.007 =$	0.00259
$n=4$	$0.10 \times 4 + 0.01$ (10-4) $0.019 =$	0.00874
$n=5$	$0.10 \times 5 + 0.01$ (10-5) $0.038 =$	0.02090
$n=6$	$0.10 \times 6 + 0.01$ (10-6) $0.063 =$	0.04032
$n=7$	$0.10 \times 7 + 0.01$ (10-7) $0.090 =$	0.06570
$n=8$	$0.10 \times 8 + 0.01$ (10-8) $0.113 =$	0.09266
$n=9$	$0.10 \times 9 + 0.01$ (10-9) $0.125 =$	$\underline{0.11375}$

$$\sum_{n=0}^{n=9} \quad sn + r(I\text{-}n)P(n) \qquad\qquad 0.34550 \text{ (accumulated total)}$$

$$\sum_{n=10}^{n=n_{max}} \quad sIP(n)0.10\times10\times0.542 \qquad = \underline{0.54200}$$

$$R(10) = 0.88750$$

$$\text{Minus } C(10) = \underline{0.50000}$$

$$N(10) = 0.38750$$

FIG. 12.4.   Value of *n* for an Inventory of 10

make each day by maintaining an inventory of 10 newspapers. But we can find that out by computing the value of n for an inventory of 10, using the model on page 150. To satisfy your curiosity, the figures are given in the table in Figure 12.4.

So long as Dick maintains an inventory of 10 newspapers to start each day, and the parameters remain the same (i.e., $s = 0.10$, $b = 0.05$, $r = 0.01$, and average demand $= 10$), he can expect to make (over the long haul) a profit of $0.3875 a day. Vary any of the parameters, however, and it's a new ball game.

13

MEETING THE DEMAND . . .

How to allocate your resources
for maximum effectiveness

Probably the most common type of problem one meets with in business or industry today is the *allocation* problem. Or it might be called a *distribution, transportation,* or *assignment* problem. But whatever its name, such a problem is characterized by the fact that a limited number of resources must be used to satisfy a number of competing demands. These demands are interdependent, so that a decision about one variable affects all the others. Any decision, therefore, must be made in terms of achieving a common objective and within limits imposed by certain common restraints.

For example, a housewife with $50 a week to spend on groceries for her family has an allocation (or distribution) problem. Her objective might be to provide her family with balanced, nutritious meals within the limitation of $50. Obviously, if she spends more on meats, she will have less to spend on vegetables, desserts, etc. And if she spends more on bread and rolls, she will have less to spend on vegetables, meats, etc. If we quantify the various elements of a balanced, nutritious diet and work out a satisfactory formula for achieving it, then consider the prices of the various foods that satisfy the formula, the problem of maximizing the objective (balanced, nutritious meals at minimum cost) can be solved scientifically.

But, of course, no housewife is likely to go through this procedure. First, the payoff is probably too small for the amount of time it would take. Second, her experience will probably enable her to arrive at a nonanalytic solution that will be good enough, even though it may not be optimum. And third, allowances have to be made for variations in taste, need for variety, etc. (If we were to proceed scientifically, of course, we would assign values to these characteristics of the problem. And in some cases there would be restrictions, or constraints. For example, the husband may insist on dessert with his evening meal, and this would affect the solution.)

However, let's focus on allocation problems more typical of business and industry. These might include the allocation of resources (men, materials, or jobs) to machines, the distribution of products from plant or plants to warehouses, the determination of warehouse locations or the selection of distributors, product mix and blending problems, production planning, scheduling, materials handling, and even the evaluation of jobs and salaries. For example, a simple allocation problem that will serve as an introduction to the subject is the one we mentioned in Chapter 3.

THE CASE OF THE
ONE-MACHINE FACTORY

In the problem beginning on page 29 we asked you to imagine that you own a factory with one machine in it that you can work a maximum of 40 hours a week. On this machine you can produce two products, A and/or B, but not both at the same time. The machine will produce 200 units of A per hour, at a profit of $7 per 100 units, or 300 units of B per hour, at a profit of $5 per 100 units. The problem was, If there is unlimited demand for each product, how much of each product should you produce each week to maximize profits? We then showed you how to make a formal mathematical statement of the problem (create a model), which was

$$P = \$7x + \$5y$$
$$\tfrac{1}{2}x + \tfrac{1}{3}y \leqq 40$$
$$x \geqq 0, y \geqq 0$$

where $x = 100$ units of A and $y = 100$ units of B. Any solution to the problem must satisfy these formulas, or constraints.

Continuing with our formulation, the classic statement of an allocation problem is

$$PX_{ij} \text{ or } CX_{ij}$$

where X_{ij} is the number of units being distributed, allocated, transported, or assigned from a supply at i to meet a demand at j, and P_{ij} or C_{ij} is the profit or cost of making such an allocation from i to j. When profit or cost is given, then total profit or cost becomes a function of X. The larger we can make X, the larger our profit will be. The most common constraints are those of supply and demand.

For example, in the case of our one-machine factory, if there were no restrictions we would produce *both* A and B in unlimited quantities (in fact, there would *be* no problem). But while there is no constraint on the source of X at i (A, B), the demand at j (the capacity of the machine) is limited to $\tfrac{1}{2}x + \tfrac{1}{3}y \leqq 40$, which means that we can produce either $80x$ or $120y$, or some combination of both. The formula $P = \$7x + \$5y$ shows us which combination would produce the most profit. And in this case it's $y = 120$, $x = 0$. We would therefore produce 12,000 units of B for a profit of $600.

THE GEOMETRIC APPROACH TO A SOLUTION

Of course, a problem as simple as this one, with only two variables (A and B), could also be solved graphically (geometrically), using the equation $P = \$7x + \$5y$ (which is a statement of the objective function) and the inequality $\frac{1}{2}x + \frac{1}{3}y \leqq 40$ (which is a statement of the production constraint). But since this problem is too simple to be typical, let's complicate it slightly by adding another constraint. This we can do by making it a two-phase operation requiring the use of another machine. If the first operation is, say, stamping, the second operation might be polishing.

We saw that the first machine takes $\frac{1}{2}$ hour to stamp out 100 units of product $A(x)$ and $\frac{1}{3}$ hour to stamp out 100 units of product B (y), and that the total machine time available each week is 40 hours (and therefore the total number of A and/or B that can be stamped out each week is limited by the constraint, $\frac{1}{2}x + \frac{1}{3}y \leqq 40$).

Let's now assume that the second machine takes $\frac{1}{4}$ hour to polish 100 units of A (x) and $\frac{2}{3}$ hour to polish 100 units of B (y), and that the total machine time available each week is also 40 hours. The total number of A and/or B that can be polished each week is

Function	Product A	Product B	Machine time available
Stamping	1/2x	1/3y	40
Polishing	1/4x	2/3y	40
Profit	7x	5y	

FIG. 13.1. Factory Problem in Tabular Form

therefore limited by the constraint, $\frac{1}{4}x + \frac{2}{3}y \leqq 40$. Our objective function ($P = \$7x + \$5y$) remains the same, but now our production problem has two constraints. In tabular form, it takes the pattern shown in Figure 13.1.

The problem remains the same: How many units of A and/or B should we (can we) produce each week to maximize profit? This problem is still simple enough to solve geometrically. All we have to do is to chart these relationships on a graph, using one axis for the y-variable and the other axis for the x-variable, both appropriately scaled. This is illustrated in Figure 13.2.

This graph tells us a number of things. First, any point that you select within the shaded area $ABCD$ will satisfy the constraints and will therefore be a feasible solution to the problem. However, the lines AD and DC, any point on which satisfies the inequalities, are the *upper* limits of production. Since these are our *only* restraints, we know that the optimum solution will be a point located *on* these lines, or as close to them as possible. All we have to do is find it.

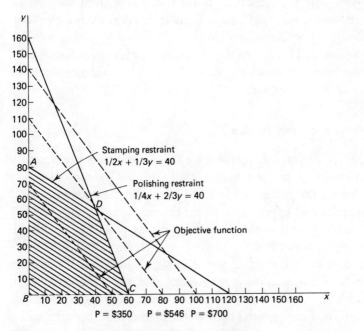

FIG. 13.2. **Graphic Solution to Factory Problem**

We do this by drawing a series of lines representing the objective function, $P = \$7x + \$5y$, and selecting that line within the area of feasible solutions that gives the highest value for P. The broken lines on the graph in Figure 13.2 are representations of this profit equation. The line $P = \$350$ is feasible, but it is low. The line $P = \$700$ is high, but it is outside the area of feasible solutions. The line $P = \$546$ just touches the area of feasible solutions at D. Since any higher value for P would take us beyond the area of feasible solutions, this is our optimum solution. That's about all there is to it.

Of course, this is a simple problem, and it is possible to express many more constraints. The net effect of such constraints would be to diminish the area of feasible solutions. In fact, there could be so many constraints that the problem might have only one solution, or even none. But what makes the geometric approach limited in its usefulness is that a graph is two-dimensional (has only two axes—one vertical and one horizontal) and is therefore limited to problems with only two variables. If we had had a third variable (a third product), we would have been in trouble. Although, theoretically, it is possible to create a three-dimensional model, it is not too practicable. This means that in more complex situations, involving more than two variables, we have to utilize other techniques in our search for a solution.

MAKING USE OF THE MATRIX

At this point you may feel that we are complicating unnecessarily an extremely simple problem, but unfortunately most allocation problems are not simple—in fact, they are extremely complex. And the formulas and approaches we are describing will give you some understanding of how the normally complex problems are solved. For example, if you had the problem of assigning 20 jobs to 5 different machines (instead of just 2 jobs to 2 machines), there are 5^{20}, or 1 trillion, possible combinations that might be considered, each with its own costs or profits to be worked out. Quite a sizable job, even for a computer! That's where mathematical programming techniques, which we are leading up to, come in. They provide important shortcuts to the answer, even though in most cases the use of a computer will still be necessary.

But, first, let's complicate our problem somewhat by adding another product (so that we have products A, B, and C) and two more machines (so that we have machines D, E, and F) to our factory and laying the problem out in the form of a matrix, such as we described in Chapter 3, pages 26–28. The payoff matrix is a useful (and in most cases a necessary) first step in the solution of an allocation problem. Figures 13.3 and 13.4 show how our matrixes would look.

Demands

	D	E	F
A	(11)	(12)	(13)
B	(21)	(22)	(23)
C	(31)	(32)	(33)

Sources (rows i), Demands (columns j)

Demands

	D	E	F
A	7	4	3
B	5	0	2
C	10	8	1

Sources (rows i), Demands (columns j)

FIG. 13.3. Matrix X_{ij} FIG. 13.4. Matrix P_{ij}

The matrix at the left represents the units to be distributed or assigned from the sources (i = A, B, C = the rows) to satisfy the demands (j = D, E, F = the columns), while the matrix at the right represents the profits that would result from such assignments. In other words, if we assigned 10 units of B to machine D in matrix X_{ij}, matrix P_{ij} shows that we would make a profit of $50 (10 × $5). However, we'd like you to imagine the boxes in matrix X_{ij} to be blank, since at this point we have assigned no values to X. The numbers that are there are for identification purposes only. They identify the particular box and apply to *any* matrix. For example, X_{23} means the value of X to be found in the second row, third column; X_{31} represents the third row, first column; etc.

Just as in our mathematical formulation of the problem, we combined X_{ij} and P_{ij} into PX_{ij}, so the two matrixes above can be combined, and usually are. Arbitrarily assigning values to X for illustration, our combined matrix might look like Figure 13.5.

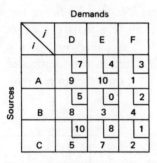

FIG. 13.5.   Matrix PX_{ij}

This, of course, could be either a solution or a proposed solution to our problem. The number in the upper right-hand corner of each box represents the profit to be made if one unit of X is transferred from the source in row i to meet the demand in column j, while the number in each box represents the units of X we propose to distribute, allocate, transport, or assign. With this information, it is easy to determine the value of PX_{ij}. For example, $PX_{23} = \$8$, the profit we shall make by assigning 4 units from B to F. The total profit which the matrix solution represents is the sum of all the squares, or

$$P = \sum_{i=1}^{3} \sum_{j=1}^{3} PX_{ij} = \$262$$

Of course, we don't know whether this is an optimum solution or not. And the matrix fails to take into account the restrictions which make the problem a problem in the first place. In matrix terminology, these restrictions are called "rim" conditions—because that is where they are written. The restrictions on demand are located at the bottom of each column in the rim of the matrix, while the limi-

To From	D	E	F	R_j
A	7 9	4 10	3 1	20
B	5 8	0 3	2 4	15
C	10 5	8 7	1 2	14
R_j	22	20	7	49 49

FIG. 13.6.   Matrix PX_{ij} with Rim Conditions

tations on sources are written in the rim at the right of each row. If our matrix were satisfying rim conditions (R_j, R_i), then it might look like Figure 13.6.

In this case, X units from sources A, B, and C (providing maximum units of 20, 15, and 14) have been so selected that they meet the demand at D, E, and F (utilizing maximum units of 22, 20, and 7)—a total of 49 units. Of course, since we don't know whether or not this is an optimum solution, or at least "good enough" (optimal), we can't really say that the problem has been solved. To do that, we turn now to a consideration of . . .

LINEAR PROGRAMMING THEORY
AND TECHNIQUES

"Linear" means "straight-line," and is descriptive of the relationship between variables. Two variables are said to have a linear relationship "if a change in one always produces a change in the second that is proportional to the change in the first. Thus, if we say $A = f(B)$, where f is a linear function, then any change in A is some constant times the change in B. An example of a linear function is $A = 3 + 0.5B$. If $B = 20$, then $A = 13$. If we double B, making it 40, then $A = 23$. If B is 10, then A equals 8. In each case, A changes by an amount of 50 percent that of the change in B. Expressed in graph form, this relationship is represented by a straight line—hence, linear. In a commercial setting, a linear situation would exist, for example, where an increase in the number of workers or machines increases production, or an increase in advertising expenditures expands product sales." *

Linear programming techniques are essentially "guided search" methods. If we could make a complete enumeration of every possible solution to an allocation problem, there wouldn't be much of a problem (we'd simply select the best solution). But even the simplest allocation problem can involve millions of possible solutions, and arriving at an optimum or "good enough" solution can be both time-consuming and tedious. Linear programming tech-

* Moshman, Jack, "Decomposition—Seven League Boots for Linear Programming," *Computers and Automation,* February, 1965.

niques narrow the search, and with the help of computers it is possible today to solve problems involving as many as 500 equations and 1,500 variables in a few hours, or even faster.

The first step in solving an allocation problem is to make a formal mathematical statement of the problem, including the objective function (to maximize profits, minimize costs, etc.) and the relevant constraints (such as limitations in supply or demand). This automatically establishes the area of feasible solutions. The search for an optimum or "good enough" solution involves applying the objective function to this area of feasible solutions, or, starting with any solution, systematically improving the solution (the objective function) until no further improvement is possible.

This is essentially what we did in solving our factory problem, using first the algebraic method and then the graphic (geometric) method. But both these methods, we saw, are restricted to very simple problems—the graphic, because it can't handle a problem with more than two or three variables, and the algebraic because it is extremely time-consuming if the problem is complex. Linear programming methods, on the other hand, can be used to solve allocation problems of any degree of complexity.

Linear programming methods fall into three or four broad categories. *Assignment* methods are used to solve allocation problems when the sources of supply (origins) exactly equal the sources of demand (destinations).* *Transportation* methods apply when the number of origins and the number of destinations are unequal. Both these methods are often lumped together as *distribution* methods. The *simplex* method (or algorithm) is more general, however, and can apply to almost any kind of allocation problem. But it usually requires the use of a computer and is used for more complex problems. Finally, a number of *approximation* methods have been developed which are useful when the problems are so complex that finding the optimum solution would be more time-consuming and expensive than it is worth, and when a reasonably good solution, quickly arrived at, would be just as feasible and possibly more economical than continuing the search for the optimum solution.

---

* That is, we have sufficient resources on hand to meet the demand, and the problem is simply how to *assign* those resources most effectively.

FIG. 13.7. Multistage Linear Problem

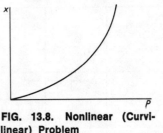

FIG. 13.8. Nonlinear (Curvilinear) Problem

Many allocation problems are of a multistage linear nature, which means that a fresh decision is called for at each stage of the problem. A technique called *dynamic programming* has proved to be useful in such situations, but it is very difficult to apply. And when relationships between variables find expression as curves, as in Figure 13.8, nonlinear, rather than linear, mathematical programming techniques are called for.

USING MATRIXES TO MAKE ASSIGNMENTS THAT MAXIMIZE RESOURCES

The first scientific techniques for solving problems in distribution, allocation, transportation, or assignment were developed during World War II, but these were difficult for anyone but a mathematician to understand. Then, in 1953, W. W. Cooper and A. Charnes developed a fairly simplified technique called the "stepping-stone" method. Subsequent modifications have taken place, but this approach is still basic to any understanding of the use of matrixes to solve allocation problems.

To show how it might work, let's return to our three-product, three-machine factory problem, but with new constraints, or rim conditions. Since origins equal destinations, this is an "assignment" problem. And the problem is: How many units of X should we assign from origins A, B, and C to destinations D, E, and F to maximize profits? Figure 13.9 shows how the matrix might look with new rim conditions and an initial, arbitrary solution.

The solution shown in this 3×3 array (three origins, three desti-

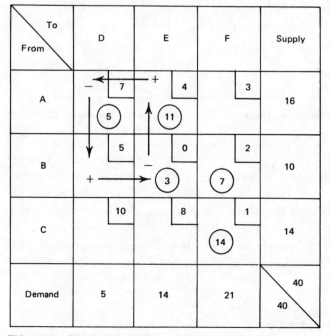

FIG. 13.9.   Distribution Matrix, Initial Northwest-corner Solution

nations) is called a "northwest corner" solution because it begins, quite arbitrarily, in the upper left-hand corner of the matrix. Square X_{11} is assigned maximum value within the constraints. In this case X_{11} is limited to 5 units by the demand at D, leaving 11 units at A to satisfy the demand at E. However, the demand at E is for 14 units, leaving an excess demand for 3 units, which we satisfy by "stepping down" to draw upon the source at B. Subtracting 3 units from a total supply of 10 at B leaves us 7 units to use in partially satisfying the demand for 21 units at F. The remaining 14 units necessary to satisfy the demand at F are then drawn from C. You'll notice that supply equals demand, and all the rim conditions are met (that is, the circled figures add up both horizontally and vertically to the sums shown in the supply rows and demand columns).

This problem is simple enough to make a good visual solution possible. For example, on inspection, it's obvious that we would do better to satisfy the demand at D from the supply at C instead of at A, to supply 3 units to meet the demand at E from C instead of from B, and to meet the demand at F by supplying 5 units from A, 10 units from B, and only 6 units from C. This solution would still satisfy the rim conditions and at the same time increase total profit from $107 (using the formula on page 162) to $159—quite a sizable increase.

However, trying to arrive at an optimum solution by visual inspection is hit-or-miss at best, and once you get beyond the more obvious improvements, particularly in a complex problem, you can waste a lot of time and never be sure you have found the optimum solution. What's needed, obviously, is a more systematic method of searching for the best solution. And that's where the stepping-stone method comes in—so-called because the circled numbers (assignments) are known as stepping-stones (the blank squares are called "water squares"). This method can be applied to allocation problems of any size and is a useful introduction to some of the other search methods, such as modified-distribution (MODI, for short), which have largely superseded it.

The technique used is called an *iterative* process. That is, it is repeated over and over until no improvement is possible—at which point you have your optimum solution. But it is both tedious and time-consuming, and after shifting assignments, previously evaluated water squares have to be re-evaluated. Fortunately, refinements in the stepping-stone method were made almost immediately, and these led, two years later (1955), to what has been called the "modified-distribution" method (MODI), which shortens the search for an optimum solution by assigning index numbers to the rows and columns. Since then more advanced techniques have been developed, but most of these are beyond the scope of this book.

OTHER METHODS BRIEFLY
CONSIDERED

Since the better the initial solution we start with, the fewer iterations we shall have to make in our search for the optimum solution, a number of *approximation* methods for solving allocation problems have been devised which yield good initial solutions. One of the most useful of these is the Vogel Approximation Method (VAM), which was devised by W. R. Vogel in 1955. VAM gives not only a good initial solution, but in most cases a solution that is optimal. This can be verified by MODI and further improved if necessary.

Another approach (the simplex) to solving allocation problems is more general in scope, and it applies to almost any problem that can be solved by mathematical (linear) programming. The name, of course, is a misnomer. The *simplex* approach (or algorithm) is rather complex and normally requires machine computation. Fortunately, the simplex method lends itself well to machine computation. The few simple formulas that the method involves are easily programmed into a computer, and the computer will save time and eliminate error. But however complex the problem, the same basic steps are involved in its solution, and applying the techniques is largely routine. The *difficult* part of the assignment is in determining the facts and setting up the problem to begin with. And which method you use will be largely determined by the problem itself.

14

HOW TO
TACKLE A SMART OPPONENT . . .

Game theory and competitive strategies

In many ways, game theory, which is concerned with risk taking in conflict situations, is the most complex, least developed, and least applicable of the many scientific decision-making techniques we have been concerned with. Yet potentially, since life, and business life in particular, is essentially a matter of conflict and competition, it could be the most important, and the most widely applicable, of the many theories we have discussed. In this chapter, therefore, we shall take a look at some of the simpler aspects of game theory as applied to conflict situations.

These are situations where, although our objective may be to maximize gains or minimize losses, we are faced with an opponent or competitor who wants to do likewise . . . and his gain is our loss, or vice versa. Therefore, in any strategy we work out, we have to take possible actions of our opponent or competitor into account. These, obviously, are game situations (hence the name), but they also include many real-life situations, such as bidding for a job, devising an advertising strategy in a limited market, working out a battle strategy, etc.

THE BASIC ELEMENTS
OF GAME THEORY

Most of the credit for the development of game theory (the application of mathematics to conflict situations) goes to John von Neumann and Oskar Morgenstern, who wrote about it in a book called *Theory of Games and Economic Behavior,* first published in 1944. They described there the basic elements that make up any conflict situation. These include the players or opponents, the rules of the game, the payoffs or outcomes resulting from any decisions, the valuations assigned to the payoffs by the different players, the variables controlled by each of the players, and the information available.

Any strategy, to be successful in a conflict or competitive situation, will usually take all these elements into account. The outcome in any game situation will depend upon the strategies employed by yourself and each of your opponents . . . and their interaction. The payoffs may be win, lose, or draw, or the loss or gain of money, prestige, etc. What is at stake is something each player values. The objective may be to maximize gains, or minimize losses, in view of the possible strategies available to an opponent whom we consider smart (or rational).

THE TWO–PERSON
ZERO–SUM GAME

The simplest type of game (or conflict situation) is that in which two opposing forces (not necessarily individuals) are involved in a situation in which the precise gains or losses of one player are the losses or gains of the opposing player. Most two-person games, or team sports, are of this nature (that is, they are either win, lose, or draw). But many real-life situations are equivalent to this. And when they are, a payoff matrix which includes the relevant features can be useful in solving them. For purposes of illustration, let's look at a rather basic example which, though not necessarily realistic, provides a useful "game" situation.

Tom Agent is fleeing a small country (where a coup d'état has put a dictator in control) with $1 million in gold coin and jewels which the dictator feels belongs to him. Tom is driving toward the border with the prize in a chest on the car seat next to him. The chest is too heavy for him to carry alone, so the money and jewels have been divided into ten approximately equal units worth $100,000 each. In case Tom has to abandon the car, he can (hopefully) carry some of the packets with him.

The border is just the other side of a river which Tom is approaching. Behind him all possible means of escape are blocked by soldiers. The border itself has not been closed off yet, though Tom has received information that Colonel Assaroff, head of the secret police, has reached the other side of the river and is waiting for him. There are two bridges across the river, an auto bridge and a railroad bridge. If Tom crosses by car and the Colonel is not waiting for him at the other end, he will get away with all the money. But

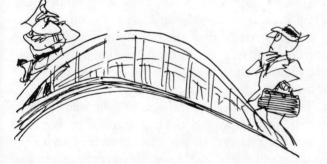

if the Colonel has set up a roadblock, Tom will have to abandon the car and escape into the woods with only two packets of money.

Tom's second choice is to cross the railroad bridge on foot along a catwalk. But in this case he will be able to carry only five packets of money. And if the Colonel has chosen to guard this escape route,

Tom will be able to save himself only by jumping into the river and swimming to shore, carrying only one packet of the money with him. The problems are: which escape route should Tom choose to maximize his gains? And, conversely, which escape route should the Colonel choose to guard to minimize his losses? In short, which of the strategies available to each of the opponents should each of them adopt in this conflict situation?

This is known as a two-person, zero-sum, finite game. It is two-person because there are only two opposing forces involved: Tom versus the Colonel. It is zero-sum, because we assume that none of the treasure will be lost or added to (i.e., whatever treasure there is stays in the game). And it is finite, because there is a limited number of strategies available to each of the opposing forces in the conflict (in this case, each player has two strategies available). These basic elements can best be depicted in what is known as . . .

THE GAME (OR PAYOFF) MATRIX

In drawing up a game, or payoff, matrix, it is customary to list the strategies available to the player with whom we identify on the left side of the matrix, and those available to the opponent on the top side of the matrix. The payoffs, indicated in each box, are considered to be gains for "our" side (if they are positive figures) and losses for the opponent. In reality, of course, a two-person, non-zero-sum game is perfectly symmetrical (that is, the two positions can be reversed, since one player's gain is the other's loss).

In the game under consideration, since we have identified with Tom, we list his strategies at the left and the Colonel's at the top of the matrix. Tom's objective is to maximize his gains; the Colonel's objective is to minimize his losses—which is simply a conventional way of looking at the problem. In this case, since they each have two strategies, this is called a "2 × 2" game. If one of the players had three or more strategies (i.e., many), it would be a "2 × m" game.

There are also 3 × 3, 3 × m, 4 × 4, and 4 × m games, etc. But each step up in the complexity of the game adds new problems, until in an infinite game like chess, where each of the players has so many different strategies available to him that they're almost

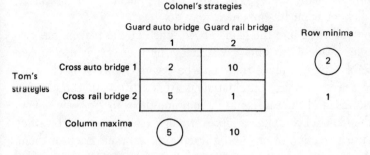

FIG. 14.1. Game Matrix for Tom and Colonel

beyond count, the complications are enormous. Let's, therefore, stick with the simple 2 × 2 game in this chapter, which will permit us to explain some of the basics of game theory with less danger of slipping in over our heads.

Figure 14.1, for example, shows how the game between Tom and the Colonel might look with all the relevant information in the form of a game matrix.

THE CHOICE OF STRATEGIES

Before we get into the choice of strategies (or how to play the game using the matrix as a model of the conflict situation), it might be best if we define some of our terms and make explicit some of the assumptions on which game theory is founded. It is assumed, first of all, that the players are rational (i.e., that each of them is trying to gain as much from the game as he *safely* can in view of the fact that he is faced with an opponent or opponents who are trying to do exactly the same thing), and that their interests are antithetical.

It is also assumed, because of the requirement that the game be played safely, that the objective of the protagonist is to maximize the *least* amount he can win, and that the objective of the antagonist is to minimize the *greatest* amount he can lose. To depart from strategies that achieve these objectives is risky for either player, and it is assumed that they will not do so. On the other hand, if each player chooses his strategy on the basis of this argument (which is central to game theory), he cannot fail to achieve his objective, regardless of what his opponent may do.

Now let's examine the game above. Each of the players has two strategies available to him. (A strategy, by the way, is a complete course of action, a move that can't be reversed once it is chosen.) These are known as "pure" strategies (i.e., they are complete in themselves, and the players can't combine them in any way). Tom and the Colonel can choose *either* strategy 1 or strategy 2, but they can't use a fraction of one and a fraction of another. Each of them, in other words, can choose either the auto bridge or the railroad bridge, but if either player decides to change his mind once he has made his move, it will be too late.

Many games, however, like flipping coins, consist of a series of moves. In such cases a mixed, or grand, strategy may be called for, which means mixing the pure strategies according to some rule (for example, choosing strategy 1 three times as often as strategy 2 over the course of play, or choosing strategy 1 on a single-play because it is three times as likely to pay off as strategy 2). In other words, this kind of strategy is a "probabilistic" mix.

If you take to heart the assumptions on which a rational game is played (and you'd better, unless you just love risky situations where the potential gain may be great but where you are likely to lose), then working out the actual play, or choice of strategies, can be quite simple. It's cut and dried, in other words. The protagonist (in this case Tom) goes along each row and picks out the minimum gains (minima) which his strategies provide, writing them in the margin (which is what we have done in Figure 14.1).

Assuming that his opponent wishes to minimize his losses, Tom goes down each column and writes in the margin the maximum which his opponent can lose by choosing each of *his* strategies. These are the maxima of his opponent. Tom then assumes that his opponent will choose that strategy which provides him with the payoff that is the minimum of his maxima (which is called his *minimax*). As for himself, Tom chooses that strategy that provides the maximum of the minimum payoffs (his *maximin*).

In the matrix of the Tom–Colonel game, Tom's maximin is 2 and the Colonel's minimax is 5 (both of which we have circled).

Both players should therefore choose their first strategy, which will result in a payoff to Tom of two units. The value of the game (as far as Tom is concerned, if he sticks to a maximin solution) is $200,000. Of course, this is decidedly unfair to the Colonel, and if Tom were a sport about it, he would spot the Colonel that amount before they began playing.

MIXED STRATEGIES AND SADDLE POINTS

Now, what mixed strategies should Tom and the Colonel pursue if this were the kind of game that was to be played over and over? This, too, is quite simple to work out. The first step is to do what we have just done in the problem above: work out the maximin and the minimax. If these are equal, then the game is said to have a *saddle point,* and the players should *not* use a mixed strategy. Instead, they should continue to use their pure strategy each time, the one dictated by their minimax or maximin.

If either player departs from this strategy, while his opponent doesn't, he will gain less from the game than he might otherwise have—and this, as we have defined the term, is irrational. To demonstrate, let's change the payoff valuations in the Tom–Colonel game to create a saddle point (the chance of a 2 × 2 matrix of random numbers having a saddle point is about 2 to 1, but this dwin-

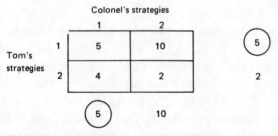

FIG. 14.2.   Game Matrix with Saddle Point

dles rapidly in larger matrixes to the point where in a 9 × 9 matrix there is only 1 chance in 1,000 of it containing a saddle point).

Examining Figure 14.2, you can see that if Tom switches to strategy 2 while his opponent continues using strategy 1, he will gain one less unit each time. If both players switch to strategy 2, Tom will gain 3 less units each time. Therefore it is clearly to his advantage to play strategy 1 *every* time. The Colonel then must assume that his opponent is rational and always play strategy 1 also. If he doesn't, but switches to his strategy 2, he will lose 10 units instead of 5 each time. This game is therefore *strictly determined* (i.e., rational players have no choice—they *must* play their pure strategy).

In the original game, the situation is quite different. While Tom can always guarantee himself a minimum gain of 2 units by playing strategy 1, by occasionally switching to strategy 2 he stands a chance of picking up 5 units instead of 2. And conversely, while the Colonel can always keep his maximum losses to 5 by playing strategy 1, by switching to strategy 2 when he thinks Tom is about to do the same he may cut his losses to 1 and at the same time keep Tom from making a gain of 3 units.

The problem for each of the players is the same: Should they occasionally switch to strategy 2, and if so how often? Or, in game language, what is the value of the game, and how can Tom best see that he gains that as a minimum and the Colonel that Tom gains it only as a maximum?

MIXED STRATEGIES AND THE VALUE OF THE GAME

When the Tom–Colonel game was played on a one-time basis, we saw that it had a value of 2 units (or $200,000), which is the value of the gain to Tom and the loss to the Colonel each time the game is played. If the game is to be played many times, however, the discrepancy between the Colonel's minimax and Tom's maximin becomes of the utmost importance. How, Tom will ask himself if he is shrewd, can he take advantage of the fact that the best the Colonel can hope to keep his losses to is 5 units? He should suspect that the true value of the game lies somewhere between 2 and 5, and that he can increase his average gain to this amount by adopting a mixed strategy (i.e., by occasionally playing strategy 2). This is what he must now work out.

Assuming that the Colonel is equally shrewd (and we normally would), he will suspect that Tom has figured this out, and he will adopt a mixed strategy of his own to counter Tom's. If either player fails to adopt a mixed strategy, he will not maximize his gains. In fact, Tom could realize average gains higher than 5, or the Colonel could realize average losses less than 2, if the other player fails to maximize his mix. But what mixed, or grand, strategy will maximize Tom's gains and minimize the Colonel's losses? In other words, what should be the ratio of strategy 1 to strategy 2 for Tom, and for the Colonel? This, too, is easy to determine.

The first step, after you have made sure that there is no saddle point, is to erase the row minima and the column maxima and forget about them. The next is to figure the absolute differences between the payoffs in each row and the absolute differences between the payoffs in each column, and write them in the margins, as in Figure 14.3.

The figures in the margins (called "oddments") indicate the odds on the different strategies, or the ratios with which they should be played—except that the oddment for the first strategy applies to the second, and vice versa. In other words, Tom's odds are 2:1 in favor of strategy 2 (i.e., he should play strategy 1 and strategy 2 in

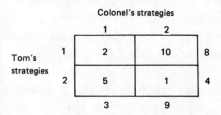

FIG. 14.3.   Game Matrix with Oddments

a ratio of 1:2), while the Colonel should play strategies 1 and 2 in a ratio of 3:1.

In a 2 × 2 game, the value of the game is always determined by the maximum mixed strategy as used against *either* pure strategy of the opponent. This is obtained by multiplying the oddment times the payoff for either of the opponent's strategies, and dividing by the sum of the oddments. For example, the average payoff for Tom, if he uses his mixed strategy and the Colonel uses pure strategy 1, is:

$$\frac{(1 \times 2) + (2 \times 5)}{1 + 2} = 4$$

Tom's mixed strategy against the Colonel's pure strategy 2 should produce the same results:

$$\frac{(1 \times 10) + (2 \times 1)}{1 + 2} = 4$$

And, of course, the Colonel's mixed strategy against either of Tom's pure strategies will produce the same result:

$$\frac{(3 \times 2) + (1 \times 10)}{3 + 1} = 4$$

$$\frac{(3 \times 5) + (1 \times 1)}{3 + 1} = 4$$

In other words, no matter how you slice it, if either of the players uses his mixed strategy, he can guarantee himself either a minimum gain of 4 or a maximum loss of 4. This is the true value of the game. This value can be altered by adding a constant to each of the payoffs, or by multiplying each of the payoffs by a positive constant; but it will not change the play of the game, since the ratios are not changed. But at this point let's quietly drop the whole subject, since the larger games become enormously complex.

In its present stage of development, game theory can be applied in only the most elementary competitive situations. In real life, much conflict takes place with little knowledge of the odds, or indeed without much of the information necessary to fully delineate the competitive situation. A salesman bidding on a contract, for instance, often will not know the *number* of his competitors, much less their identity or quoted terms. And additional factors, such as vendor reputation and past relationships between vendor and purchaser, only complicate the situation that much more.

While game theory will undoubtedly come to have increasing importance to the executive in the future, the contribution it can

make at present is probably greatest in providing a framework in which to work on these overcomplex problems that fall into the conflict category. According to J. D. Williams, "The concept of a strategy, the distinctions among players, the role of chance events, the notion of matrix representations of the payoffs, the concepts of pure and mixed strategies, and so on give valuable orientation to persons who must think about complicated conflict situations." *

* J. D. Williams, "The Compleat Strategyst, being a primer on the theory of games of strategy," McGraw-Hill Book Company, New York, 1954.

15

THE NEEDLE IN
THE HAYSTACK AND
OTHER DILEMMAS . . .

How to solve search, information, and replacement problems

We are concerned with identifying recurring problem patterns which the executive may recognize, so that he can select and apply the appropriate problem-solving strategy. While many of these strategies require extensive use of mathematics, there are also some that need very little. The following types of problems call for a wide range of techniques, ranging from the very commonplace to the highly complex:

- Most *search problems* call for finding the most efficient means of conducting a search, and the biggest job is establishing what the search problem is and what resources and methods should be used.
- *Flow-of-information problems* generally require a large, comprehensive bank of data to support various management, planning, and engineering analyses. One example is constructing an *input-*

output model, which is mostly a question of collecting and classifying raw data and forecasting volumes for the future. Another example is the *corporate model,* which utilizes the total information system of the enterprise to answer "what if" questions. The corporate model (financial model, production model, or marketing model, as it is variously known) simulates the organization and predicts the effect upon finances, sales, or operations of adopting a particular strategy.

■ *Replacement problems* call for a balancing of costs of replacing materials, parts, machines, etc., by alternative approaches—essentially a cost comparison.

It is possible to illustrate the facets of the most frequent of these problems with a proverbial search that you are unlikely to experience as an executive . . .

THE HAYSTACK PROBLEM

If you lost a rare and valuable needle in a haystack, would you take the trouble to look for it? If the needle was worth $500 and your time $25 an hour, how long a time would you spend searching for it? And how would you go about it?

Perhaps finding a needle in a haystack is easier than most people think. When you dropped the needle, you must have been at one side of the stack. It isn't likely that you could have dropped the needle above your arm level. And the needle would most likely come to rest within an inch or so of the surface. *A cursory glance in the most obvious places* could make an extensive search unnecessary—for example, you might even look for the needle glinting in the sun.

Segmenting the search area helps reduce search time. By setting aside each batch of hay that you examine, you avoid looking at the same hay repeatedly. Finally, *some special technique or device* might work magic. Sliding down the haystack would at least alert you sharply if you chanced to hit the needle. Recruiting a half-dozen small boys would extend your search capability. Best of all, a large magnet (always handy to have around) might pick up the lost needle in seconds.

While finding a needle in a haystack is hardly an executive problem, conducting a search is. Whether the prize is oil or customers or information or opportunities, the problem is much the same: how to know what you're looking for, how to organize the search, how to recognize the prize when you come upon it, and how to do

all this with the least cost in time or money. Some typical search problems are:

■ *The search for lost items* (a missing airplane, the child lost in the woods, etc.).

■ *The search for resources* (drilling for oil, researching for new chemical compounds, etc.).

■ *The search for opportunities* (seeking new markets for existing products, new areas to research for possible new products, ways to cut costs, etc.).

■ *The search for items previously stored or in hiding* (information retrieval, search to identify fugitives from justice, etc.).

■ *The search for errors or hazards* (inspection and quality control, auditing for errors, etc.).

This list could easily be extended with additional search situations, some obvious and some not so obvious. Despite appearances to the contrary, most of these searches can be tackled with quantitative methods. Search theory, for example, has enabled the military to develop procedures to minimize time loss and maximize the chance of success in a search for missing airplanes. The essential characteristic of search problems is the *need or desire to find something,* and the objective of search theory is to maximize the chance that you'll find what you're looking for with a minimum expenditure of your resources (men, money, time, etc.).

SOME VARIATIONS ON THE SEARCH THEME

Of course, not all search problems are exactly alike. The overall strategy (allocating search effort most effectively) must be varied a bit to apply to differences in the object sought, to differing probabilities that the target can be found and recognized, and to the different ways in which an object can be concealed or stored.

In some cases, the object sought is not even known. The company seeking new customers, for example, may not know their identity and location in advance. It will then be necessary to define the criteria for a desired customer: how much buying power he must have, how good a credit risk he must be, how likely he must be to make repeat purchases, etc.

Another variant is *target mobility*. If the object sought is stationary or nearly so, and on a single surface, the search can be fairly simple. The searcher sweeps the area in concentric circles or in parallel lanes. If the target is not limited to a surface (as a ship is) but can move in three dimensions (as an airplane can), the mathematics can become quite complex. If the target moves, the direction and speed will increase or decrease the chance of spotting the target at any given observation. Therefore, the *probability* that the object sought will be *in a specific location* may determine how the search should be structured. If a neighbor's bitch is in heat and your male dog gets loose, where do you look first?

Then there is *recognition probability*. Three naval aviators survived 34 harrowing days on a rubber raft in the Pacific during World War II. Ironically, a search plane passed within a half-mile of them the morning after they were downed. Evidently the tiny raft, orange-yellow in color, was obscured by the reflection of the morning sun on the water as the search planes headed east, and they failed to see it.

Failure to observe a target, or to recognize it when seen, is an error that many people cannot understand or tolerate. Yet it occurs.

In auditing, the problem of recognition errors is difficult to overcome—more so than sampling errors. The sampling error can be avoided by proper statistical methods, such as an adequate sample, well dispersed. But physical and psychological factors may prevent an auditor from realizing that he has come upon the object of his search.

Also, assuming that you can locate the target, and you do observe it as having the characteristics of the object sought, *can you positively identify it?* The hold-up victim may be able to point out the suspected robber from a police line-up—but will the identification hold up in court if, say, the suspect can produce an identical twin?

Some search problems demand only finding a *reasonable* object. The salesman who loses an order from Customer A but manages to bring in a new and better account, Customer B, may keeps his sales manager happy. But other searches require finding one specific, *unique* object. The parents whose toddler wanders away at the beach, for example, won't accept just any youngster the lifeguards find. And a missile malfunction, of course, demands finding the *exact defect.*

INFORMATION RETRIEVAL: FILE AND FIND

A complex variant of the search problem is information storage and retrieval. Any library is a storage device from which a document may be retrieved; so is a file cabinet. Whatever form it takes, the information retrieval system consists of two main activities: *file,* and *find.* Simply stated, *A* places information *B* in storage location *C* to be found by *D* for future use. Until now, we have been concerned with the second half of the search problem, the *find* portion: How does the searcher, *D,* find the object or target, *B,* in the search area, *C?* We now wish to look at the first half, the *file* portion: How does the originator, *A,* store information, *B,* in a place, *C,* in such a way as to maximize the chance that it can be found at some future date by persons unknown and for purposes unknown to the originator?

But information is a difficult commodity to classify, store, and later find. It changes with the person handling it. Let's suppose that the originator is a scientist conducting a research experiment. His findings may be of interest to other scientists, now or in the future. So may his research technique. He is willing to report his findings, possibly because he hopes to help future mankind, possibly because he wants recognition, and possibly because publication will enhance his professional status. Whatever his reason, there may be a communication gap between the research *as conducted* and *as described*. A document indexer now reads the report and classifies it as *he* sees it, using his concept of the significant descriptive terms it contains (U, V), and also according to a term describing the technique used (W). Because the indexer's thinking is different from that of the scientist, these descriptors do not perfectly portray the information in the report, much less the complete research as conducted. However described, the document is stored according to its classification, to await future inquiry.

Some time elapses, years perhaps. The potential user of the information now appears, unaware of its existence. He is looking for any previous research about a subject he describes (in terms U, X, and Y) or about a technique (Z). Again, there may be a gap between his need for information and the terms he selects to define his need. Fortunately, the system provides a cross-index that relates two of the descriptors sought $(U$ and $X)$ with the document descriptors $(U$ and $V)$, and the paper is retrieved.

The terms used to store the document must be not only comparable to terms used to find it later, but sufficiently restrictive to prevent a great number of "false-drops" from cluttering up the search. One of the problems of information retrieval is achieving a balance in using descriptors between those that are broad enough to retrieve a maximum of information and those that narrow the search by eliminating information of marginal value.

A SEARCH STRATEGY

Let's assume that you have a problem which you can now identify as "search" in nature. What is the best way to score a bull's-eye on your target?

The first step is to define the search situation:

- *What are you looking for?* How would you recognize it, if you found it? Are you looking for some unique item that you can identify, or just any item in a class of targets that will meet your requirements?
- *What is the nature of the target?* One or many objects sought? Moving or stationary? On a surface, or in three dimensions? A tangible item, or something abstract, like an idea? Does it matter *when* you find it—would its value change? Does it make a difference *where* you come across it?
- *What is the probability that the object sought will be in any given location?* What is the probability that you would observe and recognize it?
- *What is the nature of the search?* Are you trying to find the target—or to avoid it? Or do you have an object you want someone else to find? Are you concerned with the search only—or also with the method of storage or concealment that precedes the search?
- *What are the search resources?* Some searches—such as where a life is in danger—may have a time limit, because the value of the object sought drops rapidly with time. Most searches are limited by economic factors: available effort, or equipment, or money. Is there some fixed limit to your search resources?

The second step is to formulate the search method:

- *Is there some characteristic or feature that could localize the area of search?* Can you look in some obvious place first?
- *Can you organize the search in stages?* Is it possible to expend varying amounts of effort, in sequence?
- *Can you segment the search, breaking it down into manageable sections?*
- *Can you utilize some special device or technique to get the job done more effectively?*

The next step is to allocate search effort so as to find what you are seeking:

- *Is the search a simple matter, where you can use common sense to organize your resources?*

- *Or is it a complex matter, of sufficient consequence to call for a mathematical approach?* If so, you may need OR technicians to work out the optimum distribution of your search resources. In some cases, the probability of detecting the object sought is a negative exponential function of the search effort density. In other cases, where the effort has already been allocated, you may want to determine the marginal effort required to increase the detection possibility by a certain amount.

- *What equipment do you need* to conduct the search, if any?

Finally, you should know when to terminate the search:

- *Have you found what you were seeking?*

- *Or have you exhausted your resources without reaching your target?* Will you extend the search, at extra cost, or will you call it quits?

FLOW–OF–INFORMATION PROBLEMS

Like search problems, information-flow problems can frequently be tackled without recourse to complex mathematical formulas. Yet questions of how data files are to be structured, what information is to be stored, and how that information should flow to the users are essential to scientific decision-making. For unless the organization stores basic facts about its operations, it will not be able to conduct the many management, financial, and engineering analyses and the operations researches that are necessary if it is to compete in a rapidly changing world.

Most information needed to support decision-making is of three types: *routine tactical information* (to support manufacturing and sales functions, to bill the customer, to pay employees, to process returns, etc.), *routine strategic information* (periodic financial statements, regular reports of performance and progress, etc.), and *demand information* (answers to unanticipated inquiries, special reports on out-of-the-ordinary situations, and special analyses of operations).

Typical information-flow problems facing the executive are how to know what his information needs really are, how extensive the information system must be to meet those needs, how far and how fast he can afford to go in developing the system he needs, and how to design it most effectively. Unfortunately, the people who can visualize the many ramifications of information problems are in short supply, and the temptation to tackle a small piece of the basic problem often leaves the executive with an inadequate tool to support his decision-making needs.

One typical information-flow problem is organizing a materials management information system. This is more than just an inventory problem—it is often complex enough to warrant simulation on a computer of the present and future flow of materials throughout an organization, so that optimum quantities are ordered, stored, distributed, and used, so that future materials needs are projected from present usage and expected sales, and so that demand for money to pay vendors is accurately projected.

AN INFORMATION STRATEGY

Most problems about the use of information are corporate in scope: that is, they must be solved on an organization-wide basis. We shall therefore pass over the problems of how to tackle information flows of a minor nature. A suggested strategy for approaching major information problems contains three parts:

- *Definition of need*: What information is needed to carry out the objectives of the organization, when is it needed, and in what form?

- *Determination of system*: What system, equipment, and organization are required to provide the information needed?

- *Establishment of implementation plan*: What priorities and schedules are required to develop the system, equipment, and organization needed?

Designing the system is essentially a matter of organizing the flow of information most effectively. That is, the design should *minimize* movement of data *into the system* (i.e., it should eliminate duplicate recording of source data). It should *minimize* the movement of data *within the system*. Finally, it should *maximize* the timely delivery of significant information *to the end user*.

CORPORATE MODELS . . .
"WHAT IF?"

The information system can be used as a model itself, to predict what would happen to sales, operations, or finances if a given course of action were adopted.

Such a model is usually called a *corporate model, company model,* or *enterprise model.* If it deals primarily with the monetary effects of various alternatives, it may be known as a *financial model* or *economic model.* If it is concerned with corporate operations, it may be called a *production model, marketing model,* or *operations model.* Whatever the name, the nature of the model is essentially the same. The activities of the corporation (or other enterprise) are expressed as mathematical relationships. The various mathematical relationships, along with input data at specified points, constitute a representation of the corporation. This model is used in two main ways: either the input information is varied (to represent volume changes with time or other factors), or the mathematical relationships are manipulated (to reflect possible changes in the system). In this way, prospective changes can be analyzed through the use of the computer more easily and more economically than by changing the actual activities themselves.

The corporate model, therefore, can serve such purposes as the following:

Determining the effect on finances, if different levels of production or sales were assumed

Calculating how much capital would be needed, and when, to finance contemplated production

Predicting the effect of changing the prices for products or the rates for services

Determining the need for materials, fuels, etc., to support possible sales requirements or variations in the product mix

Testing the validity of proposed budgets

As a supporting tool for long-range planning

Developing the corporate model requires knowing the information to be included in the data base, determining the relationships among components of the model, and establishing control points to tie in the information system with the model. Just how effectively a "what if" question may be answered by the model depends upon the level of detail provided in the data base. Thus, the sophistication and depth of the information system are constraints limiting the use of the corporate model.

The corporate model incorporates concepts underlying various other simulations discussed in the book, but it is a macroscopic, rather than a microscopic, model. That is, *at one time* it looks at *the entire enterprise* as *an integral system.*

INPUT–OUTPUT MODELS

An extremely valuable economic tool is closely related to information-flow systems. It is input-output analysis, which constructs a model of the flow of goods and services rather than of information. The input-output model is a matrix showing the relationship between the materials and services used as *input* by the various segments of the economy and the corresponding materials and services produced as *output* by the same businesses and industries. The input-output model is used in the forecasting process to estimate the various changes to the economy and in pinpointing potential markets for various goods and services.

According to Milton L. Godfrey, formerly of EBS Management Consultants, Inc., input-output analysis can show the *direct* effect, and also many *indirect* effects, of various user purchases upon the different segments of the economy. When the consumer buys household furniture, the furniture industry feels the direct effects of this purchase; and in the input-output framework, the transportation and warehousing sector, the wholesale and retail trade sector, and the finance and insurance sector would all be directly affected by their components of the purchaser's price. The following example, provided by EBS Management Consultants, Inc., in a brochure on the subject, concentrates on the furniture manufacturing sector itself.

The furniture sector must buy a variety of materials and services in order to produce the furniture. The sectors from which these purchases are made are considered to be affected *directly* by the sale of furniture. A host of *indirect* effects will also occur from the sale of a million dollars' worth of furniture.

For example, there is the purchase of $5,150 of crude petroleum, the purchase of $56,060 of fabrics, the purchase of $1,130 of wood containers, and so on, continuing the list through all the sectors in the matrix. As a result of all these *indirect* transactions, the sectors will themselves make purchases, including possibly the purchase of furniture. Thus, because furniture is purchased by the final consumer, the furniture industry is directly affected; the furniture industry makes purchases from other industries; other industries, in turn, purchase some amount of furniture. Therefore, the total amount of furniture produced by the furniture industry is larger than the amount of furniture demanded by the final consumer, the difference being the demand for furniture that is indirectly generated. In this instance, the sale to the consumer of a million dollars' worth of furniture generates the direct purchase from the furniture industry of $551,000 worth. Then, indirectly, sales are generated for an additional $8,994 worth of furniture, a relatively small amount when compared to the amount of the direct sales.

In other types of products, the dollar value of indirect sales may be large when compared to the dollar value of direct sales. This becomes truer for industries several steps removed from the manufacture of the final product. For example, when a million dollars' worth of furniture is purchased by the final consumer, resulting in $551,000 in purchases at producer's price from the furniture industry, there are $3,875 in sales of refined petroleum products to the furniture industry. This figure is directly related to the actual making of the furniture itself. However, because of the activity generated among all the suppliers of materials and services to the furniture industry, an additional $4,883 worth of petroleum would be sold. Thus, because of this *activity* within the furniture industry, a total of $8,758 of petroleum is required.

When in addition to furniture industry activity, the activities in transportation, warehousing, etc., are considered, total sales of the petroleum refining industry caused by the sale of a million dollars worth of furniture reaches a total of $15,421, broken down as in Figure 15.1.

Thus, for the petroleum refining company, the input-output analysis provides a means for estimating the total demand for its products generated by consumer demand for various consumer goods, of which the demand for furniture is one example.

Furniture industry	$8,758.00
Other furniture and fixture industry	41.00
Transportation and warehousing	1,132.00
Retail and wholesale	5,480.00
Finance and insurance	10.00
	$15,421.00

FIG. 15.1.   Sale of Petroleum Products

This demonstration of the computed effects of the sale of a million dollars' worth of furniture to the final consumer shows the new capability provided to analysts by input-output. A relationship between final demand and the sum of direct plus indirect sales of each industry is now available to users of the input-output model.

Thus the use of input-output adds an entirely new dimension to the forecasting of sales of industrial products. The analyst for an industrial product manufacturer would develop a set of estimates for final consumption of those end products which have significant effects on his company's sales. Using the input-output tables, he would be able to compute the impact of final demand for products marketed by his company and its competitors. When used in addition to present methods for analyzing the trend of customer industries, this procedure usually results in substantial improvements in forecasts of sales of industrial goods.

REPLACEMENT PROBLEMS

When to replace equipment, people, financial support, or other resources, and *how* to replace them are common management problems and often not too complex.

Perhaps the simplest is replacement of a single machine. The problem is usually one of timing: when do maintenance and repair costs become so great that replacement of the unit is an economy? The decision means finding the optimum point in time to substitute renewed investment in equipment for increasing maintenance and repair expenses—a matter of comparing costs.

The comparison becomes complicated because it is necessary to determine the probability of repair with time. It is also complicated when the replacement equipment is more powerful or sophisticated, or of longer life, than the machine it replaces. However, there is seldom an *exact* replacement in kind: the neophyte replacing a retiring employee is of a younger generation, probably better educated, and with different social values and a different understanding of the job to be done.

Of course, the comparison may be further complicated by additional alternatives. You may consider, for example, the possibility of reducing maintenance to a bare minimum, using only enough to keep the equipment running and replacing it when it breaks down. Or you may replace certain wearing parts (e.g., the grinding heads on grinding machines), thereby prolonging the life of the total equipment with a minimum expenditure.

Where items deteriorate in value, a more complex problem is the method for replacing groups of them. Take a public utility that is required by law to test its meters every seven years. It has been established that it is easier and less costly to replace a meter and test it in the shop than to test it at its installed location. Meters, then, must be replaced every seven years, or earlier, if they fail or if customers complain about meter readings. If a meter is to be replaced (because it is seven years old), what about the next-door meter which is six years and eleven months old? Should cost of travel be considered as a factor in establishing a group-replacement policy, by area? And, if so, how far down in age is it desirable to go in establishing the replacement group?

As with complex machines, the replacement of people requires a period of parallel operation. One does not lose a controller or a plant manager one day and bring in a replacement the next. On the other hand, what is a reasonable period for training a man to replace a key executive?

REPLACEMENT STRATEGY

Most replacement problems, whether of a single item or a group of items, and whether of equipment, people, or other resources, require one main strategy: *How to minimize the sum of replacement and related costs.*

If, for example, we want to establish a policy for replacing classes of equipment that fail at different ages, we seek a solution that minimizes the total of all costs: maintenance, replacement, travel and setup, money invested, etc.

Replacement studies are primarily cost comparisons; but when more than one level of decision can be made (e.g., step up machine maintenance until complete breakdown; then consider replacing adjacent machines with like ages), other techniques can be applied.

16

SYMBOLIC LOGIC, SYSTEMS, AND CYBERNETICS . . .

**Foundations for tomorrow's world
of scientific decision-making**

Symbols, though we have tried to keep them to a minimum, are spotted throughout this book. Symbols are a kind of notational shorthand and are the language of scientists. But increasingly they will become the language of others, particularly those who must utilize

scientific methodology in the solution of problems, business or otherwise.

Symbols are primarily the language of mathematics, statistics, and logic. They are highly developed scientific tools that make it possible to manipulate our knowledge more easily, to see more clearly the relationships between facts or concepts with which we are concerned, and to arrive more easily at conclusions that are logically valid. What is more, they provide a common language that makes communication between man and man, and man and machine, easier, with less possibility of error.

Thus far we have been most concerned with the symbols of mathematics and statistics. The former are primarily concerned with concepts of quantity, the latter with concepts of probability. But there is a third type—concepts of quality and of relationships—that is of vital importance to any kind of scientific methodology. This is the subject called "symbolic logic." It is a means of stating, concisely and unambiguously, verbal propositions and their relationships. As such, it is fundamental, not only to a scientific methodology, but to any approach to "reality" that one might consider rational.

BACKGROUND OF SYMBOLIC LOGIC

Logic itself, of course, goes back to the ancient Greeks, particularly Aristotle and Thales, who apparently first conceived of the idea of generalizing experience. But in modern terms, we think of George Boole, an English mathematician, as perhaps the father of modern symbolic logic. Boole devised a system of symbols, representing propositions, which could be manipulated much like algebraic symbols to deduce logical conclusions. While Boole's original symbols have been modified and extended, Boolean algebra, as it is called, is very much with us today, finding extensive application in the design of computer circuits.

In 1910, Alfred North Whitehead and Bertrand Russell explored the foundations of mathematics in a three-volume work that is unquestionably one of the great books of our times. Called "Principia Mathematica," it is an attempt to deduce all the fundamental propositions of logic and mathematics from a small number of logical premises and primitive ideas, and by so doing prove mathematics is a development of logic. Incidental to this aim, the authors developed the notation of the Italian mathematician, Giuseppe Peano, to the point where it is a very usable symbolism. Symbolic logic and Boolean algebra have become the foundation stones for our modern world of computers and automation.

LEARNING A LITTLE OF THE LANGUAGE

Much of the difficulty one encounters initially in approaching symbolic logic lies in the fact that we are dealing with a new language. It is similar to, but not quite the same as, mathematics. Yet the reasoning processes that are involved in the two fields are very much the same. But, as Whitehead and Russell proved in their famous work, it is mathematical logic that finds its origins in philosophical logic, rather than the other way around. Fortunately, our children, raised on the new math, should have less difficulty with the language and the concepts than adults who were brought up on the "old" math. It is for the sake of these adults that we shall explore some of the basic concepts and definitions.

First of all, a distinction is drawn between symbolic logic (which is concerned with verbal propositions and their relationships) and Boolean algebra. The latter is a true algebra, but of *sets* or *classes* of elements with certain properties. It sets up certain empty forms, or generalizations, that lead to logical conclusions. And, like algebra, it obeys basic laws and has its own definitions. It is necessary to learn these if one is to understand the application of Boolean algebra and symbolic logic to specific problems. But once learned, it is easy enough to translate the symbols into the verbal language we are more familiar with, although formulating equations or following the often highly sophisticated reasoning of formal proofs or deductions (i.e., thinking in symbolic logic) may be quite another matter. This is something that might best be left to the mathematician.

THE BASICS OF BOOLEAN ALGEBRA

Basic to symbolic logic (or indeed, any logic, as Boole has pointed out) is our ability to generalize—that is, "our ability to conceive of a class, and to designate its individual members by a common name." Boole calls this operation an "election." This is done by specifying boundaries, or characteristics, that define all elements that lie within this class, or set. These elements are then designated by an "elective symbol," such as x. The universe (or "everything") from which these elements are elected is usually symbolized by the figure 1, while all else (or "nothing") is symbolized by the figure 0. The only difference today is that the elements that form classes are represented by a, b, and c rather than x, y, and z.

Boole then worked out what he called "laws of thought," or rules of operation for the use of these symbols, and adopted mathematical symbols to designate the various operations that could be performed to combine or resolve our conceptions so as to produce new conceptions involving the same elements. One of the things that makes Boolean algebra so valuable in our modern world of computer circuitry, as it turns out, is the fact that these rules of operation are the same as would apply to an algebra of the numbers 0 and 1. In short, Boolean algebra provides the basic logic for a binary system, which is the basis for many computer operations.

The two binary operations which can be used to express most of the laws, or postulates, of Boolean algebra are cup ($\cup$) and cap ($\cap$). These constitute the language of mathematical set theory. In the language of logic and engineering, these symbols would be, respectively, V,[+] and Λ, $\cdot$. It is also possible to express the postulates of Boolean algebra by means of geometric diagrams, circuit diagrams, and truth tables, where 1 = truth and 0 = falsity.

DEFINITIONS OF BOOLEAN ALGEBRA

Boolean algebra, we have seen, is a subset of symbolic logic which concerns itself with sets or classes of elements (things, ideas, etc.) which have the property of being manipulated according to certain laws. The two principal operations are ∪ (cup) and ∩ (cap). The first is somewhat analogous to arithmetical addition and may be defined as the logical sum, mathematical union, disjunction, etc., of certain sets or classes. It is also referred to as the OR operation. For example, $A \cup B$ is translated "A or B, or both."

The second operation, ∩ (cap), is somewhat analogous to arithmetical multiplication and may be defined as the logical product, mathematical intersection, conjunction, etc., of certain sets or classes. It is also referred to as the AND operation. For example, $A \cap B$ is translated "both A and B."

There are two sets of elements which satisfy the operations of both union and intersection and are known as "universal bounds." These are the universal set (1) and the null set (0). For a given set (A), $0 \leqq A \leqq 1$—that is to say, all A must equal or be greater than 0 but cannot be greater than 1. In other words, the null set is contained in A while A is contained in the universal set. If there is a union of 0 and A, and 1 and A, then $0 \cup A = A$, and $1 \cup A = 1$; while if there is an intersection of 0 and A, and 1 and A, then $0 \cap A = 0$, and $1 \cap A = A$.

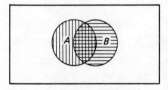

FIG. 16.1. Venn Diagram

This elementary idea will be more readily grasped, perhaps, if we illustrate it by means of a geometric, or Venn, diagram (see Chapter 7). By referring to this diagram, we can make certain statements. For example, in Figure 16.1 everything within the universal set, $1 = A \cup B$, is either A or B, or both. This includes the areas covered by the vertical lines, the horizontal lines, and the cross-hatching. The intersection of A and B $(A \cap B)$ includes the area covered by the cross-hatching only. Everything belonging to the null set (0) is outside the lined areas and contains no elements of either A or B.

The laws and the language of symbolic logic will undoubtedly have enormous importance in the future because they make it possible for computers to resolve complicated verbal relationships, such as are found in insurance policy and contract stipulations (perhaps the most successful "practical" applications to date). The design of computers utilizing the laws of symbolic logic, and the use of computers to generate truth tables from logical statements, are another important adjunct of symbolic logic.

The beauty of symbolic logic is that it makes possible the expression of complex situations and ideas in concise, unambiguous form. The disadvantages, of course, are the disadvantages of any model which is only approximate to reality. Not only that; the inherent difficulty of translating complex verbal relationships into symbolic form creates its own obstacles to practical application. Nevertheless, the advantages to the logical solutions of complex problems of conciseness, speed (utilizing computers), and accuracy far outweigh these disadvantages and hold enormous potential for the future.

TOWARD A DEFINITION OF SYSTEMS

We come now to a consideration of some concepts which provide the underpinnings and the basic framework for the revolution in scientific management that is altering not only our approaches to executive decision-making and the formulation of executive strategies, not only our working lives, but our personal lives as well. For these concepts, along with their accompanying technological discoveries, provide the foundations for automation, the more effective utilization of our resources—including manpower—in the attainment of our material goals, and the leisure inherent in the new world of tomorrow.

Basically, a system is an organized means of controlling an operation. This is the heart of the scientific approach to management and, of course, the essence of everything we have been writing about in this book. Increasingly, business and industrial operations need regulation because of the growing complexity of our technological society. The systems approach, which considers an operation as a totality, with its many ramifications and interdependencies, has developed rapidly over the past decade or two as a means of providing the needed control for complex operations. Cybernetics, carrying the approach a step further, has as its major concern the study of systems and their effective control.

Two principles that characterize effective control systems are feedback and what is called "homeostasis." The most efficient feedback is error-actuated. That is, when the system being controlled diverges in one way or another from an accepted norm, or standard, information about the divergence or error and its extent is fed back to the system so that an adjustment can be made. This property of adjusting to change and correcting for errors is known as *homeostasis*. Machine systems, such as the heating system in your home which maintains the temperature at 70° F., can have it, as well as living organisms, such as the human being, which maintains its own system at a body temperature of 98.6° F.

MANAGEMENT AND INDUSTRIAL SYSTEMS

Good management and industrial systems also have feedback and homeostasis. Such systems are becoming increasingly complex today and the need for effective control, automatic where possible, ever more urgent. Systematic management, according to one authority, "is the conscious and deliberate use of the organization, information, and techniques to plan, organize, and control the use of corporate resources in the pursuit of organizational objectives." * Without such a system, management is likely to be largely intuitive and irrational. And this is not good enough.

* Robert L. Johnson, Stanford Research Institute.

Of course, the application of the systematic approach to management is not easy, and it does not absolve management from the responsibility for its actions, such as decision-making, nor for the results. The function of management is to determine and achieve corporate, or organizational, objectives. Systems and science merely help management replace subjectivity with objectivity and the facts. And as far as possible, the systematic approach relieves the manager of routine decision-making through automation. But the risk does not entirely disappear. A good system merely helps determine the risk with greater precision, indicates which course of action is likely to be most successful, and provides more complete, more accurate, more instantaneous feedback on the extent to which objectives are being achieved.

THE IMPORTANCE OF INFORMATION

Obviously, the most important element in any system is the amount and accuracy of the relevant information it makes available on a timely basis for the purposes of control. Aspects of this problem were discussed in Chapter 8, "Concepts of Control." But information storage and retrieval, and the flow of information via a management information system, tend to be technical problems. The average executive's major concern will still be with the *use* of data to make decisions, not the *processing* of data. A good system will give him *all* the relevant data he needs to make a decision, but *only* the relevant data. This will include information from the outside world, as well as information about his own operations, and information *to* such sources to effect change.

Making it possible to receive screened, or analyzed, data on a routine basis is only one of the major advantages of an information system. But this immediately leads to a second. By knowing, and receiving, only relevant data, the executive will have a clearer idea of which decision problems can be delegated. Even more important, when the decision-making responsibility for particular problems is shifted, the information relevant to these decisions can also be shifted. And, finally, with a good management information system, it is possible to shift many routine, or programmed, decisions down to ever lower levels of the operation. Lower-echelon, or operating, people can be instructed as to the correct decision to be made in view of the feedback they receive.

DESIGNING MACHINES THAT DECIDE

Of course, when you get to the point where *people* are making automatic decisions, the question is, why not *machines?* Increasingly, systems are being designed where machines *do* make many, if not most, of the decisions. More and more, this will continue to be the case. And they will have many properties, according to Duckworth, "which are very desirable in control systems—continuous feedback, rapid response, an ability to recognize patterns better than do human beings, the capacity to explore numerous alternatives without exhaustion and so on." * In fact, they will have the capacity to do many of the kinds of decision-making that we have been discussing in this book. And eventually they are likely to have the capacity to learn, or to do most anything else we human beings program them to do.

But now we are well into the field of cybernetics proper, where in many ways the ideal computer is the human brain and the ideal machine is the human body. Cybernetics (from the Greek word "steersman"), as conceived and elaborated upon by Norbert Wiener in a book of that title in 1948, in many ways takes for granted the design of machines to do what we want them to do. Its great contribution has been to give us a new frame of reference, a new way of looking at man-machine systems and their function, that will speed the invention of the machines we need and their effective utilization within systems of control and communication. These last are key words.

* Eric Duckworth, "A Guide to Operational Research," Methuen & Co., Ltd., London, 1962.

CONTROL AND COMMUNICATION

What Wiener has asked us to do, in effect, is to view *all* systems as problems of control over living organisms and machines whose basic function is to communicate ideas and information. For example, even the automatic screw machine's prime function is to convey accurately to the metal it is processing a certain idea (i.e., the *idea* of a screw of a certain size and shape). Its effectiveness in turning out a near-perfect product will depend upon its effectiveness in communicating that idea to the metal.

"It is the purpose of Cybernetics," Wiener wrote in "The Human Use of Human Beings," "to develop a language and techniques that will enable us indeed to attack the problem of control and communication in general, but also to find the proper repertory of ideas and techniques to classify their particular manifestations under certain conditions." Two of the ideas in this repertory, we have already seen, are those of feedback and homeostasis. There are two others which are vital to an understanding of cybernetics.

ENTROPY AND NEGENTROPY

"Entropy" is the natural tendency of any closed system to become disorganized. The opposite of this is "negentropy," and this is only temporarily achieved by a system absorbing energy outside itself. Systems are islands of negentropy amidst a universal chaos. A cell, a human being, and an industrial system are all examples of negentropic systems. They are patterns of organization that persist for a time by feeding on less highly organized systems.

Cells, human beings, and industrial systems are viable systems if they appear to be purposive, that is, to achieve goals. Yet all such systems eventually run down and fail (i.e., achieve equilibrium). This is illustrated by a large container of gases of different temperatures. If there is no energy input from without the system, there will be a flow of energy (i.e., heat) within the system from areas of high temperature to areas of low temperature until the temperature within the system is equalized. (This, of course, is the Second Law of Thermodynamics.) When the system reaches a state of utter stability, it is, to all intents and purposes, dead.

We achieve purposive activity by the flow of energy or information within a system. The system perpetuates itself by absorbing energy from outside itself and affects the environment by giving energy to the environment. However, in order to continue as a viable system, the system must be adaptive and self-regulating. Most natural systems have these qualities. They achieve them through feedback and homeostasis. A major concern of the cybernetician is understanding and devising man-machine systems with these qualities.

THE "BLACK BOX" PRINCIPLE

Cybernetics is particularly well suited to deal with complex, high-variety systems. However, we must remember that most systems are of this nature—even the lowly amoeba, for instance. For example, imagine a system consisting of five units, among which information or energy must flow in order for the system to be viable. These could be five managers running a company, or five nodes in an electronic system. If each unit communicates with each of the other units, then there are 20 (5×4) one-way channels of communication. If each of these channels has the capacity to be open or closed (on or off), that is, in two states, then the number of possible states in this system is 2^{20}, or almost 2,500,000. And this is a simple system (the human brain, for instance, is estimated to have 10 billion neurons!).

If even such a simple system is found to have a high degree of complexity, how is the cybernetician or manager to deal with any system? Certainly not by the process of enumeration. The answer is ingeniously simple: one does not have to know what is going on within the system. It is enough to know the inputs to the system, the outputs from the system, and the relationships between them to effectively control the system. In other words, the system is looked upon as a "black box."

One "black box" with which most people are familiar is their own automobile. Few people know what goes on under the hood, but this doesn't stop them from being able to control the car. They know that if they turn on the key, step on the gas, etc., they are going to get certain predictable outputs which enable them to manipulate and control the vehicle so that it achieves goals they want it to achieve. In the same way, the human brain, an urban community, an industrial unit, or a complicated machine can each be operated and controlled on the "black box" principle.

INFORMATION THEORY

Because of the importance of information to cybernetics and computer systems, information theory, though still in its infancy and with few industrial applications, has come to be an increasing concern of the operations researcher and the systems analyst. As with the other theories and techniques discussed in this book, it is essentially quantitative analysis, but this time applied to communications. Much of information theory stems from work done by Claude Shannon of the Bell Telephone Laboratories in the late 1930s.

The quantification of information is based upon a number of findings or assumptions. The first of these, and perhaps the most important, is that the minimum quantity of information that can be communicated is a "bit." This bit of information tells us one thing we didn't know before—yes or no, on or off, true or false, etc. Most sentences, or other modes of communication, convey several bits of information. But if no bit has been communicated, there has in effect been *no* communication. In short, if we haven't learned something, no information has been transmitted; it is just noise.

The mathematical expression of information theory is based upon three findings by Shannon. First, the maximum rate at which information can flow through a communications system is not arbitrary; it depends upon the properties of the system and can be determined. Second, information flowing within a system is not randomly distributed or entirely independent; some information can be expected with a greater frequency than other information. Third, any communications system will always contain random interference, or noise, in its channels.

Shannon's findings have found greatest application in the design of telephone circuits, but the general principles have application to almost every other kind of communications system, including such systems within a company, and undoubtedly greater and greater use will be made of them. It is theoretically possible to determine the maximum rate of information flow within a system, the degree of error, and the amount of redundancy that must be built into the system to ensure minimum ambiguity. Also, within any communications system there is an expected loss of information which must be faced realistically.

That information theory is important to cybernetics is obvious. The control of any system depends upon the amount and quality of the information flowing within the system, and in mathematical terms it is proportional to the logarithm of the information in the system. How much and what kind of information we need to control any system is one of the basic problems of cybernetics. The further development of information theory promises to help the cybernetician solve this basic problem, which will in turn give the executive the means of improving his organization's performance.

17

FORMULATING
YOUR EXECUTIVE STRATEGY . . .

**How to get the most out of
the decision-making process**

We said at the start, you may recall, that decision-making lies at the heart of the executive function, and that a better understanding of the decision process could therefore add to one's effectiveness as an executive. We have not meant to imply that the process is a simple one, although the book contains some obvious oversimplifications for the sake of explanation. Certainly the task of recognizing problems amid uncertainty, then exploring possible solutions to the point of seeing them implemented, is anything but easy.

President John F. Kennedy spoke of "the dark and tangled stretches in the decision-making process." The newer, quantitative decision aids—operations research, probability theory, simulation of operations, and other management sciences—are making it possible to illuminate some of these dark stretches. And developing a strategy that will help shed some light on the executive's decision process has been the principal purpose of this book.

There is, of course, no single prescription that will serve as a general strategy for all decisions or for every executive. Each individual will be comfortable with a decision strategy only if it is

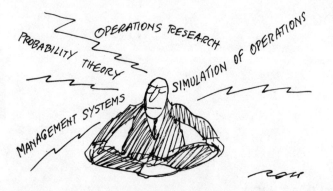

geared to his particular level, and to his personal attitudes and style of dealing with people and situations. But it is our hope that this book has presented some guidelines that will help the executive to broaden his own rationale for decision-making. Essentially, these guides tell *how an executive can concentrate his decision resources at an effective level, how to recognize situations where scientific analysis may reduce decision hazards,* and *where and when to go for help* in developing and implementing solutions.

THE DISCIPLINE OF OPERATING AT AN EXECUTIVE LEVEL

As a start, consider the level at which an executive can operate, if he will. He would like to concentrate his energies on broad policy matters, but unfortunately, routine questions constantly intrude upon his time. It is only by self-discipline that he can find the time to define problems and instruct subordinates, yet these steps are prerequisite to delegation.

As one cornerstone of an executive strategy, therefore, it will pay you to concentrate on those activities that will best discharge your responsibilities. In effect, you are allocating your most valuable executive resource—*your time*—among competing demands, and you wish to optimize your effectiveness. You should:

■ Select problems that involve *large sums of money*, and leave to subordinates those of minor economic impact.

■ Select problems that are *first of many*—nonprogrammed, generic situations for which you can establish a goal or a rule or a policy—leaving to others the minor one-time, nonrecurring problems. This step will take many individual demands for decisions out of your hands and refer them to the precedents you have set.

■ Select problems involving *design or redesign of a system*, setting the parameters by which performance is to be measured and leaving to others the decisions needed to operate the system.

■ Set aside time for the *guidance of subordinates*. This will make your delegation more effective.

■ Take time specifically to *visit the scene of action*—to make sure that the assumptions upon which your decisions have been based are really valid.

■ Reserve some time to seek out *new and potential problem situations*, to seek *opportunities*, and to *re-examine the priorities* for your time involvement.

A STRATEGY FOR SPOTTING PROBLEM PATTERNS

We have said that an executive will be better able to know what to do about a problem if he can detect the underlying pattern. If a school needs to determine how many teachers to employ for the coming school year, it will help to view the task as an inventory problem, rather than a question of education or a personnel problem. The basic problem is clearly one of how many teachers to "stockpile" to meet future demand (incoming students). The basic inventory strategy can be applied (minimize the sum of the cost of carrying too many teachers, plus the cost attributable to delays, etc., from having too few teachers). Consideration should be given to lead time (How long does it take to obtain new teachers, both before and after the school year starts?), purchasing costs (cost of recruitment), reorder point (optimum time to recruit), and similar matters.

For the reader's convenience in developing his decision strategy, Chapter 18, "Strategy Briefs for Executive Action," contains a checklist of patterns for problems that frequently recur, with the underlying management science strategy for tackling each of them.

WHEN AND WHERE TO GO FOR HELP

In putting your strategy to work, the first step is acknowledging that you need help from others. For one thing, *you are not an expert* in all areas. If you were, you would not be an executive. *Nor do you have the time.* Your own time, which is your most valuable resource, should be allocated to those opportunities and problems that are most meaningful for your organization. Yet pressures of time leave many executives with only two recourses: either to put aside time-consuming problems until they must be treated on a fire-fighting basis, or else to make snap decisions on an intuitive basis.

It is the function of staff analysts, consultants, and the like, to extend the executive's capacity to tackle problems for which he lacks either time or specialized knowledge. Both internal and external specialists serve to multiply his "thinking resources," so that his problem-solving potential is now limited only by the number of experts he can effectively work with. (You will note that we use the term "consultant," or outside professional, to include not only management consultants but also educators and specialists from accounting firms, computer software services, research institutes, and other advisory organizations.)

Where to obtain assistance is really a two-pronged question: Do you turn to people inside your organization or outside (or both)? and What kind of specialist do you need?

THE APPROPRIATE DISCIPLINE

Assigning analytical tasks to specific individuals or groups is a primary responsibility, one which distinguishes today's executive from his predecessors. With the act of choosing the appropriate "thinking resource" he has delegated some of his decision-making authority and has identified the group that is to carry the ball. When you consider that decision-making is generally the last function to be so delegated, it is obvious that the executive process has reached comparative maturity. The distinguishing feature of OR, systems analysis, organization planning, and other such disciplines is that responsibility is now designated for *analyzing* operations, not just for performing them.

The line between any two disciplines frequently blurs—the similarities are greater than the differences. The same steps are basic to most problem-solving disciplines. The differences are chiefly in the kinds of *models* that are constructed, the *techniques* for developing solutions, and (to a lesser degree) the *methods* of analysis. A listing of some of these disciplines that constitute knowledge resources for the executive is contained in "Some Further Reading," at the end of the book.

INSIDE OR OUT?

You have a choice of internal or external resources (or some combination of these) for *any* problem situation, *whether or not you have a present capability in your organization.* Each problem or opportunity presents anew the question of where to turn for help. Some considerations to take into account are:

- If you have an internal staff group, does it include people who are capable of tackling this assignment? And do they have time available?
- Even with an internal capability, would it pay to turn to outside assistance anyway, to get the job done faster? Or more effectively? Or because the problem is too sensitive (such as a reorganization)? Or to reinforce a finding by your internal staff?
- If you don't have a present capability, do you want consultants to do the entire job? Or to help you set up your own staff?
- Is this a situation where you want a joint effort, utilizing your staff to work with consultants?

In turning for help to either the consultant or the management scientist on your staff, you should bear in mind the need for considerable understanding on *both* sides. You should know enough about the techniques discussed in this book to help spot and define the problem, to follow the progress of the study, and to weigh the alternatives presented. And you should expect the specialist, in return, to be willing to consider a problem from the management point of view and to discuss facets of the problem without resorting to the jargon of his trade.

YOUR OBLIGATION TO PARTICIPATE

Effectively, you are already a participant once someone brings you a problem or you recognize an opportunity or you acknowledge a situation that might be worth exploring via the management sciences. You will no doubt want to stay with the problem until it has been re-evaluated and redefined by the subordinates or specialists who are going to work on it, to make sure that they are in agreement on what the real problem is. Unfortunately, a few executives have a tendency to then sit back and wait for the "solutions," upon which they will base their final decisions—either because of the pressure of other matters or because they may not feel "qualified" to get involved. At this point it may be too late to reshape the entire study if it happens to have somehow gotten off on the wrong track.

Your continuing participation in the study and analysis of a problem situation or improvement opportunity does not demand your involvement in the technical side of the study—even if you have the scientific background that makes this possible. But it does mean that you should obtain sufficient feedback so that you know where the study is going and what is being done. Most consulting firms give their clients status reports on a monthly or bimonthly basis, indicating such things as progress to date relative to schedule, costs relative to estimates, changes in the study approach, etc. It will pay to request the same kind of status reports from any project leader on your staff (even though your own people are on a regular salary basis), supplementing these reports with personal reviews when you feel that they are necessary for your own enlightenment, at the same time letting the project leader know that you are available when *he* has questions.

Aside from your own participation in any study for which you bear the ultimate responsibility, participation by *operating* managers is often overlooked. This is particularly unfortunate when any changes that occur as a result of the study affect the line manager's department. For one thing, knowing the functioning of his own department, he may spot errors or warn of hazards that the specialist, unacquainted with many details of the business, may overlook. For another, when the line manager has been asked for his ideas in developing a solution or specifying the problem, he is more likely to be persuaded of the validity and usefulness of the study. And both you and the specialist will have less of a job "selling" the recommended solution to those who will be asked to put it into effect.

YOUR FURTHER OBLIGATIONS AS EXECUTIVE

The executive-specialist relationship is a two-way street. You, too, have obligations in support of the professional's efforts. First, of course, is your participation, which we have already mentioned, and which is a subtle way for you to tell him that you expect performance.

You should not hesitate to make estimates or to indicate preferred approaches. Many factors are quantifiable only by value judgments, and you as an executive can help by assigning values where you are the logical one to do so. For example, you have asked for a study to improve service to the customer. The specialist can put a price tag on the changes needed to reduce the time (by X days) and improve quality (by raising the rejection rate Y percent), but he comes to you for your estimate of the value of these benefits (e.g., How much is better customer good will worth—what would you spend to placate an offended customer?). In Chapter 3 we indicated how you might use the standard gamble to "measure the unmeasurable."

You will want to provide access to operational people. Analysts and consultants cannot verify your assumptions, or obtain valid data, if their contact is restricted to you and other decision-makers. They need to talk with line supervisors and those who actually perform the work, if they are to understand and solve the underlying problem.

Some professionals are fast in their thinking and will propose solutions early; others are detail-minded, needing more and more corroborative facts. Frequently it is the executive who must maintain a balance, by indicating the extent of detail he considers appropriate, or by coupling the "detail man" with the "broad-brush artist" on a joint study team.

One caution: avoid overenthusiasm about advanced scientific techniques. This may sound strange, in a book on scientific decision-making. But an excess of zeal can be almost as harmful as a reluctance to try new approaches. A good executive will maintain a "controlled warmth" for these decision tools partway between the extremes of negativism (where he won't try anything) and overenthusiasm (where he occasionally needs to be "unsold").

WHAT YOU SHOULD EXPECT OF THE SPECIALIST

The good specialist will identify with your management concerns and interests and point of view. If an insider, he should think of himself (and be encouraged to think of himself) as a member of management. If an outsider, he should be clearly aware that his success as a consultant requires that the organization derive some benefit from his service. This means that he should be at least as concerned with the *management* aspects of a problem as he is with the particular *technique* he might use. He should apply his skill in order to solve *your* problem—not use your problem to sharpen *his* skill.

As a professional, the specialist should know when to cut the study off. This usually means concluding somewhere short of perfection. It is often painful for the specialist to recommend a "reasonably good" course of action when he feels that only a little additional time would permit him to come up with the "one best" solution. As the executive concerned, you may need to judge whether the cost of further refinement is worth the marginal improvement that is possible.

The truly management-oriented specialist is willing to commit himself to a preferred choice of action. As the executive responsible for that choice, you have a right to insist that the specialist do more than dump the whole problem in your lap. You should demand that he rank alternative solutions in order of preference, and that he spell out his opinion of the action to be taken.

Hopefully, he will be "management-articulate." That is, he should be able to explain his approach in the language of his client (avoiding jargon and using a minimum of formulas), whether by written report or in an informal discussion or in a full-fledged presentation. He should provide adequate documentation to describe what has been done, and what needs to be done, in terms that operational people can understand without reference to complex formulas.

Finally, the specialist should make himself available to help implement a course of action that has been decided upon, even though this may include instances where his recommended solution has been modified or even rejected.

CALLING IN A CONSULTANT

Most executives today get their first taste of scientific decision-making as applied to their own operational problems by calling in a consultant. Utilizing consultants can be a rewarding experience or a frustrating one, depending upon the client-consultant relationship that is established. To get the relationship off to a good start, it is essential that both parties understand the scope of the assignment *in advance*. And this means defining the objectives of the assignment, the extent of the work to be performed, and the fees to be paid—before work is begun.

Consulting fees, of course, can be on a fixed-fee *or* time basis. A fixed-fee assignment can be hazardous, unless the scope of the work has been carefully defined in advance (for example, it could lead to corner-cutting if consulting personnel run into obstacles and get behind in their work). The time basis, on the other hand, can lead to a never-ending assignment. One useful variant, therefore, is a time contract with a stated maximum for the project. But whatever the basis for the fee, there is less apt to be difficulty if you meet with the consultant regularly to discuss what has been accomplished and what remains to be done.

At first glance, consulting fees may seem high (time charges calculated on an hourly basis may seem to run as much as three times the hourly pay of staff employees). But the comparison is not valid, for an hour of a consultant's time is generally worth a good deal more than an hour of an employee's time. With experience in solving your type of problem in various organizations, the consultant should be able to work faster and more effectively and, what is more important, be more likely to arrive at accurate and workable solutions. In addition, you pay only for productive performance on your problem, since you are not billed for vacations, holidays, illness, professional training, etc.

Several techniques can help you get the most benefit for your consulting dollar:

- Whenever possible, use a consultant to guide internal staff personnel in conducting an assignment, rather than bring in a large consulting team to do the whole job. This will require an experienced consultant rather than a junior, but such a man can coach your team to do the job, at less overall cost, and help develop your internal staff at the same time.

- Whenever possible, assign someone as liaison to arrange appointments and make requests for data needed. This will save substantial consulting time and will lead to better relations.

- In all cases, sit down with the consulting firm's partner or principal in advance and discuss with him the objectives of the study, as you see them, and what the scope of the assignment should be. Have him specify his study method, the caliber of individuals he will assign, and complete details of fees to be charged. Ask for a written proposal spelling out these essentials and do not engage the consultant until you are in agreement on them.

- In all cases, arrange for some kind of periodic reporting of progress, allowing for immediate contact in the event that either you or the consultant requires it. A progress report should contain information about achievement of planned subgoals and about actual expenditures relative to estimates—enough so that you can tell whether or not the study is proceeding satisfactorily. You may wish to ask the consultant to specify the content, frequency, and form of such a report as part of his proposal.

SETTING UP YOUR OWN STAFF

Chances are the time will come when you will want to consider setting up your own staff to carry out projects in the management sciences. When that happens, you will want to define the group's objectives and recruit a staff, provide support, and follow up the progress of the work.

Objectives for the new function can be defined in fairly general terms (such as "Improve the effectiveness of operations") so long as specific subgoals are also named (e.g., "Improve Process Y during the next calendar year in order to reduce costs in Division C by $X"). Spelling out the particular area of competence (e.g., operations research, management systems, etc.) may seem to confine the group's activities, but it is needed to provide a focus for attracting personnel and building a project workload.

Recruitment of staff is critical, because success is a function of the ability of staff members to think and to effectively translate their ideas into completed projects. The major skills are *analytic* (to break down a problem), *creative* (to build solutions), and *communicative* (to work with people, "sell" solutions, and obtain implementation).

The key man—you may call him "project leader" or "department head"—should be selected first. He needs the same analytic, creative, and communicative skills as members of the staff, plus an ability to organize and direct the work of others. He will deal with other executives and set the "tone" of the group: choose him with care.

The support you provide is evidenced by many things, starting with where you locate the function in the organization. Have it report to the top man, say educators and consultants, in respect to almost *any* decision discipline. And this advice is usually well taken: *Functions that support decision-making should report to decision-makers.* A top executive should be willing to deal with several thinking-resource groups, along with his operating functions. In World War II, the British made effective use of military operations research groups headed by brigadiers and colonels. Because these officers were highly placed, they had easy access to policy-makers. The British OR teams came up with ways to use radar, shipping convoys, and air strength to best advantage, thus helping to stave off disaster at sea and in the air.

The internal group needs continuing support: educational encouragement, attendance at professional meetings, and library facilities. They should not be weighted down with many "fire-fighting" assignments (although a few are unavoidable—even helpful in promoting the function).

Some say that the new function should start with a relatively easy, noncontroversial project, one that will demonstrate its skills. A small initial success not only serves as a showpiece, but also builds the self-confidence of the group. If the "start small" approach is taken, it's important to avoid confining the group to small, "firefighting" projects and to move them up to larger projects that are meaningful to the organization as a whole.

Sooner or later there will be challenges from other members of your organization with respect to the effectiveness of the new group. To counter this, it's important that you, as the responsible executive, stay on top of their assignments, keeping a record of work completed, with estimated savings or other benefits. Because it takes time to set up an effective decision-making team, many department heads will be fearful and critical of the changes you are trying to effect. Thus, a record of accomplishment can be useful in the event that sniping occurs.

THE LONG AND THE SHORT OF IT

In putting his strategy to work, the typical executive is faced with both long- and short-range aspects of a problem or an opportunity. Many executives tend to focus their efforts on one *or* the other (but not both).

Whichever your style, you should consciously seek a balance.

That is, if you are generally concerned with the immediate considerations of a problem, try to get a long-range thinker to supplement your approach to decision-making. On the other hand, if you naturally gravitate to underlying problems with solutions years ahead, find someone who will worry about the immediate consequences.

Take, for example, the company that is about to acquire a subsidiary. The short-range thinker will be concerned with immediate problems, such as what he needs to do on takeover day to process the subsidiary's accounts, to deposit receivables, and to announce the acquisition to the new employees and new customers. The long-range thinker may be interested in such matters as integrating the operations of the subsidiary with those of the parent company, building new markets, and developing new products so that profit margins will be better five years from now than they are today.

In working with a specialist, whether staff personnel or consultant, it's well to know which type *you* are, and which type you are dealing with. If you're both cut from the same cloth, there's a chance you'll overlook some important aspects of the problem that confronts you. Know yourself and your counterpart, and you'll be able to make up for each other's shortcomings. In other words, if you strive for a balanced decision-making team, you'll be more effective.

HOW WELL DOES YOUR EXECUTIVE STRATEGY WORK?

Whether you, and the team you use, are effective or not will not be known with any degree of precision unless you keep close check on the progress made. This means periodically asking yourself: How effective have my decisions been? Looking back at each project you've assigned to your internal staff or to consultants, have you been reasonably pleased with the results? Or were you disappointed in the way a project turned out? How close have your projects come to meeting their estimates of time, cost, and accomplishment? It is only by reviewing your progress (and that of your decision-making team) once or twice a year at a minimum that you can improve your ability as a decision-maker.

This, especially today, is of the utmost importance. Like it or not, the world of the executive is changing. You and your associates are increasingly under pressure from competition, competition that is optimizing its own decisions by utilizing concepts and techniques we have described in this book. Therefore your own decisions need to be sharper than ever before, which means that you will want to make increasing use of the management sciences to enhance the operations of your organization. At the very least, this means an understanding of your own thinking process, an ability to recognize those situations where quantitative methods can cut the risk of error, and a knowledge of when and how to put scientific decision-making to good use. If this book has helped you achieve those ends, you will emerge a surer executive, more aware of the executive function and more confident that the decisions you reach will benefit your organization. In short, you will be a better executive strategist.

18

STRATEGY
BRIEFS FOR EXECUTIVE ACTION . . .

How to identify problems that can be solved
with management science techniques

We have said that an executive will be better able to know what
to do about a problem if he can detect the underlying pattern. If
you need to recruit employees, for example, it will help to view the
task as a *search* problem rather than as simply a personnel problem.
Questions of where to look, and how extensive your recruiting drive
should be, are easier to decide in terms of the search objective—
allocating your search resources so as to maximize your chance of
finding the people you need—and by reference to the various steps
of the search strategy mentioned in Chapter 15.

For the reader's convenience in developing his decision strategy,
we have assembled a checklist of patterns for problems that frequently recur, with the underlying strategy for tackling each of
them as developed in the previous chapters.

INVENTORY PROBLEMS

How to spot
the inventory
pattern

- The basic question is always, *How much?* E.g., how much inventory do we need to meet future demand?
- Can be applied to *any* resource (materials, manpower, money, ideas, etc.) to be stockpiled against anticipated demand.
- Subsidiary question is, *When?* E.g., what is best time to order, and in what quantities?

Typical inventory
problems

- Inventory of finished goods for sale.
- Raw materials inventory, for manufacturing needs.
- Roster of scientists needed for research laboratory.
- How much cash to keep in banks to meet anticipated demands for payment (to vendors, employees, stockholders, etc.) less expected receipts (from customers).
- How many schoolrooms, teachers, books, etc., to provide for future student enrollment.

Facets of the
problem

- *Too much inventory* means *excessive carrying costs* (cost of storing, cost of money, and cost of spoilage, obsolescence, etc.).

Inventory　　　Demand　　　Carrying costs

- *Too little inventory* results in lost sales or delays in production, thus creating *costs attributable to outages.*

Basic strategy

- *Balance too much versus too little. That is, minimize the sum of carrying costs plus outage costs.*

Inventory   Demand   Outage costs

Complications

- Each separate size and type of an inventory item is a separate inventory in itself (it's possible to have outages in individual items despite ample *total* inventories).
- Determining *when to reorder,* and *economic order quantity,* are subject to many variables: fluctuating *demand, delivery time, cost of money* (interest that could be earned if money were not invested in inventory), *space and other holding costs,* and *purchasing expense,* as well as *cost of material.*

Techniques available

- Mathematical models.
- Economic-ordering-quantity formulas.
- Computer systems for materials management (purchasing, storing, receiving, paying for, and accounting for materials) permit closer matching of inventory levels to anticipated demand, by more accurate knowledge of current and past usage.

WAITING–LINE PROBLEMS

How to spot a waiting-line pattern	▪ A waiting line is a *discipline* for providing *service to customers* who arrive at random. ▪ You may have a problem of *delay to customers,* if service is inadequate. ▪ Or a problem of *idle facilities,* if service is more than customers need. ▪ The basic question is *time.* (When do we get service, how long to get waited on, how often do customers arrive, how long must service facilities stand idle?)
Typical waiting-line problems	▪ Customers at a check-out counter. ▪ Airplanes waiting to land. ▪ Papers in your "In" basket. ▪ Trucks to be loaded. ▪ Telephone calls for a busy extension. ▪ Components awaiting final assembly.
Facets of the problem	▪ Delay to customers can be costly, if service is inadequate. ▪ Idle service facilities can be costly, too.
Basic strategy	▪ *Balance the service provided versus hazard of delay. That is, minimize the sum of cost of delay to customers plus cost of idle facilities.* ▪ Look at the *service facilities:* —Can you cut service time? —Or variations in service time? —Can you increase the number of service channels? —Or reduce the number of phases? ▪ Look at the *customer arrivals:* —Can you reduce the arrival rate? —Or vary the arrival times? —Can you break up batches of customers arriving together? —Can you predict the rate at which customers arrive, and therefore prepare for them?

Complications

- Instead of the usual first-in, first-out discipline, some waiting lines are last-in, first-out (goods stacked in a warehouse, for example).
- Impatient customers may desert the line.
- Unstable queues, where confined customers get restless.
- Arriving customers may be limited, resulting in finite waiting lines rather than infinite ones.

Techniques available

- Queuing theory (complex mathematics).
- Monte Carlo technique (a method using random numbers to simulate chance occurrences, such as arrival rates).

ALLOCATION (DISTRIBUTION) PROBLEMS

How to spot the allocation pattern

- You have resources (materials, manpower, money, facilities, etc.) to allocate among a number of competing demands.
- You want to make the allocation in the most effective manner: to maximize benefits, minimize costs, etc.

Typical allocation problems

- Assigning salesmen to territories.
- Distributing products from plants to warehouses to users.
- Setting up pipelines to and from refineries.
- Allotting funds for research projects.
- Allocating machines and manpower to work on production orders, when orders exceed available time and equipment.

Facets of the problem

- Too broad an allocation of resources reduces the extent of satisfying any given demand.
- Too narrow an allocation restricts the number of demands that may be satisfied.

Basic strategy

- *Optimize achievement of desired objectives by the most effective allocation of resources among competing demands.*

Complications

- In some cases, there is only one resource required per demand: these are *assignment* problems. For example, only one classroom may be required for assignment of a pupil in an elementary school; only one territory may be assigned to a salesman in Company X.
- A more complex problem is allocating more than one resource per demand, or more than one demand per resource. For example, assigning graduate students to various classes; or allocating territories to salesmen at Company Y, where one man may sell a line of products over many territories and where a

territory may accommodate several salesmen.
- Allocation problems grow more complex where not enough resources are available to satisfy existing demand. For example, available congressional funds are insufficient for the many projects requested by executive departments of the government.
- In some cases, resources can be increased or disposed of to match growth or shrinkage of demand. For example, Company Z can resort to financing for research projects that are beyond its present means; or it might close warehouses that are obsolete when air shipments direct from plant to user become economically feasible.

Techniques available
- Linear programming methods:
  - —Assignment methods (resources equal demands, or sources equal destinations).
  - —Transportation methods (resources and demands are unequal).
  - —Simplex method (computer approach, applicable to complex allocation problems).
  - —Approximation methods (such as Cooper and Charnes' stepping-stones method, the MODI or modified-distribution method, the VAM or Vogel approximation method, and iterative approaches).
- Dynamic programming.
- Nonlinear programming.

SEARCH PROBLEMS

How to spot the
search pattern
- Something is lost or missing.
- You need some resource.
- You are seeking opportunities.
- You want to detect errors or hazards.
- You need something previously stored.

Typical search
problems
- Drilling for oil.
- Research to develop new products or services, new product uses, or new markets.
- Auditing procedures.
- Information retrieval.
- Safety programs.

Facets of the
problem
- The search should not begin before the *nature of the object sought* and the *means of recognizing it* are defined.
- Effectiveness of the search depends upon *resources that can be mobilized* for the search effort, *the probabilities that the target will be in a given location* and *recognized when seen,* and the ways the object sought can be *concealed or stored.*

Basic strategy
- *Maximize the possibility of finding and recognizing and identifying the object sought by organizing and using search resources in the most effective manner.*
- Define the search situation:
  —What are you looking for?
  —What is the nature of the target?
  —What is the possibility that it will be in any given location?
  —What is the nature of the search?
  —What resources can you bring to bear?
- Formulate the search method:
  —Can you localize the area of search, or identify the obvious place to look first?
  —Can you organize the search in successive stages?

—Can you break it up into manageable segments?

—Can you utilize some special device or technique?

- Allocate the search effort:

—Distribute your search effort to find what you are seeking, using OR techniques if needed.

- Know when to terminate the search:

—Have you found what you were looking for?

—Or have you exhausted your search efforts?

. . . Will you marginally extend the search, or call it quits?

Complications

- The object sought may not even be known.
- The target may be either *unique,* or *one of many.*
- The target may move, in relation to the searcher.
- The target may be maneuvered to *avoid* the searcher (this is, in effect, a two-person game).
- Some search problems—like information retrieval—include consideration of the method of *concealment or storage.*

Techniques available

- Mathematical models.
- Search and detection theory.

CONTROL PROBLEMS

How to spot the
control pattern

- You want to "get things done."
- You need a system that will:
  —Alert you when a decision is needed.
  —Help determine what kind of decision should be made.
  —Help put the decision to work.

Typical control
problems

- *Tactical controls:* a steering mechanism, a heat control, a time clock.
- *Managerial controls:* quality control, PERT networks, departmental budgets, project management.
- *Strategic controls:* long-range planning, sales quotas.

Facets of the
problem

- A small signal can control vast amounts of energy, materials, or information.
- For control to work, four basic elements must be present:
  —*Input* (plans, standards, or objectives defining what must be done).
  —*Output* (what is being accomplished).
  —*Feedback* (information comparing output with input).
  —*Action* (to correct deviations or errors so as to produce the output desired; or possibly to modify the input).

Basic strategy

- *Construct a control, which will be a model of the system it is to govern.*
- *Decide on a plan or standard of what is to be achieved by the system.*
- *Provide means for measuring what is accomplished and for feeding back information about any deviation from the plan.*
- *Provide for automatic action to correct the deviation (in a closed control system) or for someone to take corrective action (in an open control system).*

Complications

- The control model must be an accurate and timely representation of the system it is designed to govern.
- The control should not be too costly, complex, or cumbersome for the system.
- Factors selected to be controlled should be critical ones, not of secondary importance.
- In utilizing controls, it is frequently better to rely upon optimum data rather than averages.

Techniques available

- Cybernetics (science of communication and control).
- Queuing theory.
- Network analysis (CPM, PERT, etc.).
- Managerial controls (budgets, progress reports, cost accounting, procedural manuals, etc.).

COMPETITIVE PROBLEMS

How to spot the competitive pattern	■ You want to succeed at risk-taking in a conflict situation: —By maximizing your payoffs and your chances of winning. —Or by minimizing your losses.
Typical competitive problems	■ Bidding for a contract. ■ Pricing your products or services. ■ Devising an advertising plan in a limited market. ■ Mounting an attack on enemy forces.
Facets of the problem	■ Number of competitors, players, or opponents. ■ Rules of the game. ■ Payoffs or outcomes desired. ■ Variations in valuation of the payoffs by competitors. ■ Variables controlled by competitors. ■ Information available to the competitors.
Basic strategy	■ *Maximize the chance of achieving desired payoffs (to win, or to minimize losses, or to pursue a mixed strategy) by:* *—Formulating matrixes listing payoffs for various strategies available to each competitor.* *—Choosing those strategies that offer the best chance of success.*
Complications	■ Competitors may not always make rational choices. ■ "Nature" (e.g., the weather) may be considered an opponent.
Techniques available	■ Game theory. ■ Construction of models of choices: —Payoff matrixes. —Graphic analyses. —Algebraic analyses. —Iterative methods (trial and error). ■ Probability theory.

INFORMATION PROBLEMS

How to spot
the information
pattern

- You need various types of information to support your operating activities and management decisions.
- What is the best way to have this information flow to you:
  —What information should be stored?
  —How should the information files be structured?
  —What system can provide the information needed? What equipment and personnel are needed for the information system? How can the system best be designed and put to work?
- Are you proceeding too fast or too slow in developing your information systems? Which of your organization's functions should be included?

Typical information
problems

- Providing tactical information:
  —Billing the customer.
  —Keeping track of inventories.
  —Answers to routine inquiries.
  —Paying employees.
- Providing strategic information:
  —Periodic financial reports.
  —Reports of performance and progress.
- Providing information on demand:
  —Supporting unanticipated management inquiries.
  —Supporting research into operations.
  —Special reports on extraordinary situations.
- Providing a combination of tactical, strategic, and demand information:
  —A comprehensive information system for materials management.
  —A management information system supporting overall needs of the entire organization, at various levels.

Facets of the problem	■ Developing a system to support the needs of an isolated function ignores the needs of other functions and results in duplicate and expensive record-keeping. ■ Developing a comprehensive system to meet all needs is a complex task. It is difficult and costly to complete, but it provides the information needed to manage the organization effectively. ■ Designing the system is a problem of optimizing the organization of information. The design should *minimize* the reentry of overlapping source data and the movement of data within the system; it should *maximize* the timely delivery of significant information to the end user.
Basic strategy	■ *Define objectives of the organization and the information to carry out these objectives.* ■ *Determine the system, equipment, and organization to provide the required information.* ■ *Establish priorities and schedules to design, develop, and install the systems needed.*
Complications	■ Changing management requirements (caused by a dynamic economy, competitive factors, and a developing science) call for redefinition of information needs and modification of systems. ■ Difficulty for internal management to have a confident knowledge of the appropriate rate of development of information systems, or the appropriate extent, depth, and format of the data to be provided.
Techniques available	■ Information theory. ■ Systems analysis. ■ Equipment analysis (including computers and data communications devices). ■ Input-output models. ■ Corporate models (financial models, marketing models, production models, etc.)

REPLACEMENT PROBLEMS

How to spot replacement patterns	■ You need to decide *when* to replace resources (equipment, people, vendors, financial sources, etc.). ■ You need to decide *how* to replace these resources most effectively.
Typical replacement problems	■ Replacing a single machine. ■ Finding a successor to a retiring supervisor. ■ Developing a source of supply to replace an unsatisfactory vendor. ■ Replacing a group or class of parts, facilities, etc.
Facets of the problem	■ Early replacement increases investment and the cost of money. ■ Late replacement may cause delays and increases the cost of maintenance and repair.
Basic strategy	■ *Balance costs of early replacement against late replacement. That is, minimize the sum of all replacement costs: investment and money costs; maintenance and repair costs; cost of delays; travel and setup costs; etc.*
Complications	■ In real life, the replacement is seldom exactly the same as the resource it succeeds: —Replacement machines are faster, more powerful, with greater capacity, require less space, etc. —The new employee brings social and educational abilities different from his predecessor's. ■ The cost of money changes with time. ■ Items can be replaced in whole or in part, singly or in groups. ■ Replacement may require testing and/or a period of parallel operation.

Techniques
available

- Cost comparisons.
- Value theory.
- Probability theory.
- MAPI (Machinery and Allied Products Institute) formula.
- Monte Carlo technique.

SOME FURTHER READING

It may be that you may wish to refer to some more authoritative source, either to pursue a particular problem further or to develop a deeper knowledge of the management sciences.

The following list contains a few books that we considered of more than passing interest and, in the case of search theory, a three-article series by Koopman which is still an authoritative work in this little-documented field.

This list is far from being a complete bibliography of the literature in the field or even of the good books. They are simply works that the authors have found readable and well written, and that touch on various aspects of management science. They range from the less difficult ("A Manager's Guide to Operations Research," "The New Science of Management Decisions," "The Human Use of Human Beings," etc.) through to a few of the most difficult ("An Investigation of the Laws of Thought," "Principia Mathematica," "Theory of Games and Economic Behavior," and "The Mathematical Theory of Communication").

The most difficult books are listed, first, because some of them are classics, and second, because glancing at them will give you some idea of the true difficulty inherent in the subject matter. This will counter any impression our own essentially simplistic overview may have given you that management science is either easy to understand or easy to apply. It is a field that requires true expertise, yet there are rewards for the executive who knows enough about the subject to know when to call in the expert and how to work with him effectively.

Ackoff, Russell L., Shiv R. Gupta, and J. Sayer Minas: "Scientific Method," John Wiley & Sons, Inc., New York, 1962.

————, and Patrick Rivett: "A Manager's Guide to Operations Research," John Wiley & Sons, Inc., New York, 1963.

Adler, Irving: "Probability and Statistics for Everyman," The New American Library, Inc., New York, 1963.

Beer, Stafford: "Decision and Control," John Wiley & Sons, Inc., New York, 1966.

Boole, George: "An Investigation of the Laws of Thought," London, 1854 (reprinted by Dover Publications, Inc., New York, 1959).

Charnes, A., W. W. Cooper, and A. Henderson: "An Introduction to Linear Programming," John Wiley & Sons, Inc., New York, 1953.

Churchman, C. West, Russell L. Ackoff, and E. Leonard Arnoff: "Introduction to Operations Research," John Wiley & Sons, Inc., New York, 1957.

Dantzig, George B.: "Linear Programming and Extensions," Princeton University Press, Princeton, N.J., 1963.

Dewey, John: "How We Think," D. C. Heath and Company, Boston, 1910.

Dodgson, Rev. Charles Lutwidge (Lewis Carroll): "Symbolic Logic" (available in paperback edition from Dover Publications, Inc., New York).

Drucker, Peter F.: "Managing for Results," Harper & Row, Publishers, Incorporated, New York, 1964.

————: "The Practice of Management," Harper & Row, Publishers, Incorporated, New York, 1954.

Duckworth, Eric: "A Guide to Operational Research," Methuen & Co., Ltd., London, 1962.

Eddison, R. T., K. Pennycuick, and B. H. P. Rivett: "Operational Research in Management," English Universities Press, 1961; John Wiley & Sons, Inc., New York, 1962.

Fetter, Robert B., and Winston C. Dalleck: "Decision Models for Inventory Management," Richard D. Irwin, Inc., Homewood, Ill., 1961.

Flagle, Charles D., William H. Huggins, and Robert H. Roy: "Operations Research and Systems Engineering," The Johns Hopkins Press, Baltimore, 1960.

Gass, S. I.: "Linear Programming," McGraw-Hill Book Company, New York, 1958.

Goldman, Stanford: "Information Theory," Prentice-Hall, Inc., Englewood Cliffs, N.J., 1953.

Goode, Harry H., and Robert E. Machol, "System Engineering," McGraw-Hill Book Company, New York, 1957.

Grawoig, Dennis E., "Decision Mathematics," McGraw-Hill Book Company, New York, 1967.

Hilton, Alice Mary: "Logic, Computing Machines, and Automation," Spartan Books, Washington, 1963.

Johnson, Richard A., Freemont E. Kast, and James E. Rosenzweig: "The Theory and Management of Systems," McGraw-Hill Book Company, New York, 1963.

Koopman, Bernard O.: "The Theory of Search," *The Journal of the Operations Research Society of America;* in three articles:
    I. "Kinematic Bases," June, 1956.
    II. "Target Detection," October, 1956.
    III. "The Optimum Distribution of Searching Effort," October, 1957.

Koopmans, Tjalling C., ed.: "Activity Analysis of Production and Allocation," John Wiley & Sons, Inc., New York, 1951.

Levin, Richard I., and Charles A. Kirkpatrick: "Planning and Control with PERT/CPM," McGraw-Hill Book Company, New York, 1966.

Magee, John P.: "Production Planning and Inventory Control," McGraw-Hill Book Company, New York, 1958.

March, James G., and Herbert A. Simon: "Organizations," John Wiley & Sons, Inc., New York, 1958.

McGregor, Douglas: "The Human Side of Enterprise," McGraw-Hill Book Company, New York, 1960.

Metzger, Robert W.: "Elementary Mathematical Programming," John Wiley & Sons, Inc., New York, 1958.

Miller, David W., and Martin K. Starr: "Executive Decisions and Operations Research," Prentice-Hall, Inc., Englewood Cliffs, N.J., 1960.

—— and ——: "The Structure of Human Decisions," Prentice-Hall, Inc., Englewood Cliffs, N.J., 1967.

Moroney, M. J.: "Facts from Figures," Penguin Books, Inc., Baltimore, 1951.

Morse, Philip M., and George E. Kimball: "Methods of Operations Research," John Wiley & Sons, Inc., New York, 1951.

Newman, William H., and Charles E. Summer, Jr.: "The Process of Management," Prentice-Hall, Inc., Englewood Cliffs, N.J., 1961.

Sasieni, Maurice, Arthur Yaspan, and Lawrence Friedman: "Operations Research, Methods and Problems," John Wiley & Sons, Inc., New York, 1959.

Schlaifer, R.: "Probability and Statistics for Business Decisions," McGraw-Hill Book Company, New York, 1959.

Shannon, Claude, and Warren Weaver: "The Mathematical Theory of Communication," The University of Illinois Press, Urbana, Ill., 1949.

Shuchman, A.: "Scientific Decision Making in Business," Holt, Rinehart and Winston, Inc., New York, 1963.

Simon, H. A.: "The New Science of Management Decisions," Harper & Row, Publishers, Incorporated, New York, 1960.

Steel, Robert G. D., and James H. Torrie: "Principles and Procedures of Statistics," McGraw-Hill Book Company, New York, 1960.

Truxal, J. G.: "Automatic Feedback Control System Synthesis," McGraw-Hill Book Company, New York, 1955.

von Neumann, John, and Oskar Morgenstern: "Theory of Games and Economic Behavior," Princeton University Press, Princeton, N.J., 1947.

Whitehead, Alfred North, and Bertrand Russell: "Principia Mathematica," Cambridge University Press, London, 1910, 1912, 1913.

Wiener, Norbert: "Cybernetics," The M.I.T. Press, Cambridge, Mass., 1948.

————: "The Human Use of Human Beings," Houghton Mifflin Company, Boston, 1954.

Williams, J. D.: "The Compleat Strategyst," McGraw-Hill Book Company, New York, 1954.

INDEX